PARK CITY Underfoot

SELF-GUIDED TOURS OF HISTORIC NEIGHBORHOODS

D1566111

PARK CITY Under Foot

SELF-GUIDED TOURS OF HISTORIC NEIGHBORHOODS

BRENT CORCORAN

SIGNATURE BOOKS
SALT LAKE CITY, UTAH

To Colleen McDannell
from her laziest student
and in memory of Mara Altaveer
who would have agreed with her

Thanks to Linda Thatcher of the Utah State Historical Society Library and staff of the State Office of Historic Preservation, as well as to the staff of Special Collections, Marriott Library, University of Utah.

Martha Sonntag Bradley both read and undertook the tours and offered helpful additional information and revisions. John Keahey and Allen Roberts kindly volunteered to read and revise the manuscript. Ravell Call provided artistic photographic perspectives; Keiko Jones produced the hand-drawn maps.

Cover design by Julie Easton

99   98   97   96   95   6   5   4   3   2   1

Library of Congress Cataloging-in-Publication Data
Corcoran, Brent
Park City underfoot : self-guided tours of historic neighborhoods
/ Brent Corcoran.
    p. cm.
ISBN 1-56085-065-5
1. Park City (Utah)—Tours. 2. Historic Sites—Utah—Park City—
Guidebooks.   I. Title.
F834.P3C67   1995
917.92'14—dc20   94-36029
                                                CIP

Contents

Preface

Park City is an oasis of sorts—a splash of color on a monochromatic cultural canvas. "In Utah, but not of it," residents say. Compare, for example, Salt Lake City's gridiron pattern of streets oriented around the imposing Mormon temple, symbol of eternal order, to Park City's streets which evolved helter-skelter according to mountain topography and proximity to worldly mines. Kin-based populations in the state's valleys remained stable for decades, while Park City's transient populace, victim of the vagaries of the free market, ebbed and flowed. This once-secluded cleft in the Wasatch Range continues as a respite for seekers of diversity.

Despite significant growth in recent decades, Park City still feels like a small town. Commercial zones blend easily with residential areas; condominium complexes and restaurants share compatible architectural plans and materials. Unlike larger metropolises where crowded downtown areas compete with rambling suburbs, here inner and outer quadrants interconnect easily. The streets are usually safe, and exploring back alleys can be delightful, as can relaxing in alpine meadows within easy walking distance of Old Town.

As you make your way along the following walking and bicycling tours, remember that historic buildings and houses are labeled according to their original designations rather than current ownership and are given contemporary names only where convenient for orientation. Be advised that businesses come and go, that restaurant hours are seasonal, that many shops close in May and October, and that houses can change color. Once you settle into the relatively casual pace, you should find it enjoyable.

Park City Underfoot is not a comprehensive history or almanac, nor a promotional tract, of which there are already several. Here, Park City's story is told in relation to physical history, the background given for each significant residence, saloon, church, or mercantile at the location where these intriguing events occurred. If I have done justice—both to the human and the sublime—readers should be able to visualize and appreciate better this community's colorful legacy.

Introduction

Ever since the founding in 1872 of this mining-turned-skiing boomtown, Park City residents have been self-conscious about their relationship to their western neighbors. In the mid-nineteenth century Mormons left an American Babylon to forge a perfect society near the protective peaks of the Rocky Mountains. Park City's original leaders came west to get rich, challenging what they considered to be the quaint and insular culture of the Mormons. Park City's history was capital-driven. Its historic residents were investors, management, and labor. Parkites dreamed big dreams, made and spent big money, and fought big lawsuits.

Mormons knew early on that the mountains held considerable mineral wealth. One of the first claims in the area was staked by Mormon leader Parley P. Pratt. Soon after their arrival in the Great Basin, Brigham Young organized exploration parties to assess the region's resources, not in quest of gold and silver which had little practical value but the way to independence and perfection through pursuit of agricultural riches. "Let the gold be!" he commanded. The invasion of Mormon Utah by outsiders posed a threat to the unity of the Saints. The ragged hoards of '49ers who passed through the territory on their way to the California gold fields two years after Mormons arrived were evidence of the folly of terrestrial pursuits.

Federal officials worried that an economically independent Mormon society would become a politically independent one. Fearing a theocratic empire beyond federal control, in 1857 the government sent troops to Utah to put down Mormon rule. Mormons had already displayed an unwelcoming posture toward federal bureaucratic and judicial representatives—many of whom fled the territory within months of their appointments. The short-lived Utah War guaranteed that the territory would stay within federal control. When Colonel Patrick Connor later led a Union army to Utah in 1862 to establish a permanent military presence, he and his troops were largely ignored.

Connor's army was recruited from veterans of California's gold fields. Since Mormons weren't in a fighting mood, and his troops were restless, Connor let them do what they liked best. Soon army prospectors swarmed nearby hills and discovered silver across the mountain from Park City in Big Cottonwood Canyon at what would become the world-famous Emma Lode. When the first claim was declared in the Park City area in 1868, the floodgates to fortune hunters burst wide open. A town was soon born.

Establishment of a mining industry was the first substantive blow to Mormon automony. In 1869 another blow to Mormon independence fell when railroad companies joined their transcontinental tracks at Promontory Point, Utah Territory. Easy cross-country travel forced

Mormons to meet the world but ensured the success of the infant mining industry. Transportation was essential to satisfy the mines' and mills' need for fuel and to haul away processed metals and ore to market. Railroading and mining grew, if not harmoniously, at least interdependently.

During the early camp years miners' houses and small-time businesses lined the road leading to the first paying mine: the Ontario. Later called Main Street, this road was cleared and graded to provide access to Ontario Canyon. Park City developed along this central corridor. With growth, streets on both sides parallel to Main Street gradually moved up the slopes of the mountains.

Park City, like most mining towns, soon played out its surface ores, the small-timer's easy pickings. The real wealth was buried deep and could only be had for real money.

One of the first big investors in Park City was George Hearst, William Randolph ("Citizen Kane") Hearst's father. Robert Chambers headed his Park City interests. Edward Ferry led another investor group out of upstate Michigan. Although Chambers stayed aloof from the ragtag community, Ferry and company threw their weight around. They recognized that the town's residents were technically squatters without legal claim to town lots and schemed to acquire the townsite patent and then sell the land back to those who already had houses and businesses there. The deal didn't go unchallenged by Parkites. But the "Michigan Bunch" won. The townsite scandal was a lurid tale of payoffs, double-crosses, and legal shenanigans that lasted thirty years. Even today muddy historical land titles can lead to legal problems.

Park City encountered equal difficulty in the process of incorporation. Town governments had to solicit authority from the territorial government to oversee police, fire, utility, tax, and local ordinance legislation, and Mormon territorial officials were reluctant to grant charters to fly-by-night mining camps, especially gentile-owned ones. But legislators could not ignore the ten-year-old, 4,000-member community. Eventually a city charter was granted. Then more problems arose when the city held two competing elections. Two factions fought over the legitimacy of ballots, but neither was valid. Amid national clamor for family values that year, the U.S. Congress invalidated all elections held in polygamous Utah Territory. The town did not receive a legitimate city government until 1884.

The city continued to grow and, unlike other mining boomtowns, had staying power. Despite the occasional shoot-out through Main Street's swinging saloon doors, Park City was like most other frontier towns. The number of churches, schools, and fraternal orders speaks to the development of a real community. But compared to most Mormon farming communities, the Park's population was in flux, buildings came and went in succession, businessmen wandered between retail and office spaces, miners rented rooms rather than buy houses, and mining claims changed hands almost daily. The economy depended on precious metal prices and railroad power plays, and as the national economy fluctuated so did the fortunes of the Park.

The ethnicity of the city's immigrant population followed national trends. In the early years immigrants were primarily northern European—British, Irish, German, and Scandinavian. The sizable Chinese community, drawn from railroad labor, was the exception. In the 1900s and 1910s southern Europeans arrived, including Italians, Spaniards, and Slavs. Each group had its own residential enclave, its own saloons, its own specialized occupations. Living patterns tell a lot about a town's social fabric. Park City was a loose ethnic confederacy at best. The Chinese, for example, were relegated to a ghetto in the ravine behind Main Street and worked as cooks, laundrymen, and at times porters. The Irish lived in boarding houses and ran saloons. The Scandinavians lived in other boarding houses and cut lumber. Germans lived in company-owned houses and hotels and were often mining engineers. The British rented houses and supervised the mines, whereas American-born residents owned both houses and mines.

At heart the immigrants were quintessential Americans, driven by a common dream of property, opportunity, and happiness. But it took a tragedy to bring them together to cross carefully-drawn lines and to realize their shared values. On 19 June 1898 a devastating fire obliterated the greater part of town. Parkites heroically put aside enmities and worked together to rebuild. The only outcasts were the ones who threw up their hands and abandoned town altogether. Lessons learned after the fire would be remembered during future booms and busts.

The conflagration was a historic watershed in other ways. The turn of the century saw greater consolidation of the town's principal industry as companies bought, merged with, or drove out competitors. Out of hundreds, three major companies survived, and these final three eventually merged into one. Mining, which started as a pick-and-shovel business, came to demand greater technology as ore became more inaccessible. Greater resources demanded greater capital. By the 1950s Park City had become a one-company town.

Finally, even the impressive conglomerative capital was played out. Residents feared that their community was destined for membership in the bittersweet fraternity of western ghost towns. Where Park City once proclaimed itself the virtual county seat, county officials now left it off maps entirely. The town that once lorded its wealth and sophistication over rural neighbors looked with longing at the prosperous dairy farms in nearby Snyderville. Years passed when the only trade in town was moving people out. The newspaper noted a real estate purchase as a major event, while houses stood empty and businesses were boarded up. Soon all that changed.

Like Park City, Aspen, Colorado, was another mining boomtown close to becoming a ghost town. But capital and vision transformed it into a world-class ski resort playground, a living set for lifestyles of the rich and famous. Some in Park City determined that if such success could happen there it could happen here. During the 1960s and 1970s investors leveled a ski slope, built a lift and, for good measure, a lodge. Then capital arrived. Within ten years Parkites went from complaining about the glut in real estate to moaning about soaring prices.

Park City today is an internationally renowned resort town and tourists, the city's economic lifeblood, can expect to be pampered. But Park City's permanent inhabitants, like other resort town residents, suffer mixed emotions when it comes to their part-time neighbors. Imagine having house guests who stay half the year. On the other hand, ten-year residents are considered old-timers. People quickly develop a sense of community and behave like an extended family. They squabble among themselves, but woe to the outsider who criticizes.

Development is the town's major preoccupation and it places real power in the hands of city planners and bureaucrats. Developers, like tourists, are considered necessary evils. Residents want progress, but they can't agree on how to define or control it. A property owner's rights are balanced with the impact on neighboring properties.

Somehow Parkites take this all in stride. They endure the busts and manage the booms. When skiing arrived in a big way, the newspaper ran regular features on the winter sport to acclimate residents. City planners embraced historic preservation as part of their promotional vision. Visitors encounter a thriving, high-tech town not knowing that locals marvelled at their first traffic light only thirty years ago. The town that couldn't make it on the map is now site of the 2002 International Winter Olympics.

Individualistic, outward-looking, and progressive, Park City faces another booming century.

Architectural Styles, Plans, and Construction

Park City's early residents were poor and needed cheap, no-frills housing. Built of wood—a handy, relatively low-tech medium compared to brick or stone—most of these temporary houses contained four rooms or less. These quaint historic residences now stand in stark contrast to modern alpine retreats. Although mine owners left a legacy of opulence both here and in Salt Lake City, only three of their mansions have survived in Park City.

The simplest miner's shack was constructed like a box. Framing was minimal and consisted of horizontal planks used for support against vertical boards forming the walls. Doors and windows were cut out of the self-contained box. Builders with more resources and expertise who erected vertical-stud frames still used rough boards for walls. Even the interior walls lacked lathe and plaster.

Among Park City's historic architecture, three vernacular plans dominated distinct time periods with some overlap in popularity. Architects use the term vernacular to describe folk plans, styles, and methods of construction—the types of buildings erected by those without special training. The earliest were simply rectangular houses. These were the first permanent shelters, replacing tents and shanties. During its heyday, 1870-90, builders placed two unevenly-sized rooms broadside to the street to give the illusion of spaciousness with two windows surrounding a central door to create a symmetrical façade. They used single-wall construction for most rectangular houses, the structure of the building forming the interior wall as well.

The crosswing cottage enjoyed popularity between 1880 and 1900. Builders placed two wings at right angles, sometimes achieving a full T and other times simply an L, with the door placed close inside the cross. Whereas rectangular houses were cautiously symmetrical, crosswing cottages were more rambling, picturesque, "romantic." Rectangular houses were at times remodeled by adding a stemwing perpendicular toward the street, thus creating the vernacular form known as "crosswing cottage by addition."

Parkites turned to classical, four-square plan cottages around 1890-1910. Four-square plans were often topped by a pyramid-shaped roof, particularly useful in a snowy mountain town. The roofs were often truncated or hipped. This was not a complete return to the rectangular house since the door, because of variations within the larger four-square plan house's interior room division, could be placed asymetrically off-center. Interior rooms varied in size. Also, the house could be embellished with Victorian details like lathed poles and gingerbread wood shapes. Sturdy frames allowed for a second story. Crosswing cottages were sometimes remodeled into four-square plans by adding rooms between the stem and wings.

The last historical plan was the bungalow, favored throughout the years 1900-20 when taste vacillated again toward the picturesque. Bungalows are relatively rare in Park City because their heyday corresponded to a low period in the city's economic history. Besides the bungalow, Park City missed out on several other subsequent trends in American residential architecture over the next several decades because of the area's depressed economy and peculiar topography. Few period revival cottages or Frank Lloyd Wright-inspired Prairie bungalows are found in or nearby Park City. Nor will one find any early-modern International Style structures.

Since the Park's renaissance as an upscale ski resort community, modern architectural styles have flourished in the hills above the historic district. Many of these vacation homes are influenced by multilevel California Style, designed to accommodate hillside sites. Another popular plan is the A-frame, ubiquitous to American resort communities. The first A-frame was designed by a Wright draftsman, Rudolph Schindler, who, while working in California's Lake Arrowhead community, was able to convince city planners that the unusual structure fit within their guidelines for "Norman Style" houses.

Park City's commercial structures can be traced back no earlier than the 1898 fire which all but decimated the business district. Immediately thereafter merchants built typically Victorian mining-town structures. A simple wood-frame building with a steep roof was hidden behind a flat-topped, street-side façade.

At the turn of the century commercial façades were decorated with wood cornices, and indented entranceways were placed between two display windows. Transoms began appearing over doors and windows, and stone and brick buildings emerged with an occasional arch, Queen Anne-style brickwork, or columns and piers.

After Park City's 1960s rebirth, city planners envisioned one general style of commercial architecture that could lend itself to different interpretations. Officials used the term "Park City Style" when putting forth their architectural vision. They believed this would help achieve some kind of continuity in commercial districts. Ideally, buildings in Historic Commercial Zones were to recall, but not necessarily replicate, the city's boomtown Victorian structures. Today two primary examples of this Park City Style can be found at either end of Main Street: the loose interpretation featured in the Main Street Marketplace Mall and the more derivative look of the Summit Watch Development.

WALKING TOURS

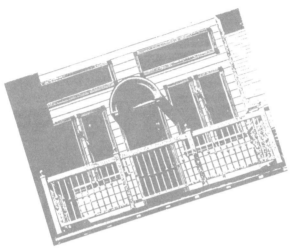

I.
Main Street

DISTANCE: 1 MILE   TIME: 4 HOURS

This tour takes visitors down the east side of historic Main Street to the Summit Watch Development, across Main Street, and back up the west side of the street. A municipal parking lot south of the Wasatch Brew Pub (250 Main Street) is accessible from Swede Alley which parallels Main Street to the east. There is also multi-level parking at 400 Swede Alley.

In the 1870s Main Street was an aspen-lined dirt track leading to mines in Woodside, Empire, and Ontario canyons. While miners lived in boarding houses and cabins near mine and mill sites, merchants settled more centrally here, a pattern that persisted.

A century later, in 1973 city officials accented Main Street's western look with board sidewalks, gas lamps, and western-style marquee signs. Every summer the street is blocked off for a weekend to accommodate the Park City Arts Festival which Jim Patterson and Mike Dontje inaugurated in 1970. The first festival attracted 7,500 people and sixty-seven exhibitors. Today's festivals are so congested that many locals abandon town during the event. Another festivity is the 4th of July parade which has been a major event since mining days when it was a worker's only summer holiday. International attention is drawn to Main Street every January by Robert Redford's Sundance Film Festival. Thousands attend the independent film premiers.

The tour begins at the Wasatch Brew Pub.

1. Wasatch Brew Pub (250 Main Street)

Tourists rave about Utah's landscapes and complain about its confusing liquor laws. In 1917 Utah led the nation into Prohibition by two years, and today take-home sales of wine, strong beer (anything over 3.2 percent alcohol), and distilled drinks are handled exclusively by state-run liquor stores. Restaurants and hotels serve alcohol from midday to midnight only and are required to use regulated measuring dispensers.

In spite of this, at least six microbreweries now thrive in the state. Whereas major out-of-state breweries are compelled to dilute most of their beer prior to shipping to Utah, the state's microbreweries target 3.2 levels as the end-product and serve it straight from the tap.

One of the Park's first brewers, Greg Schirf, began in 1986 to produce the popular Wasatch Ale brands which include stouts, bocks, and lagers. He later expanded operations with a 13,000-square-foot brewery in the Salt Lake Valley, tripling output. The Wasatch Brew Pub

MAIN STREET

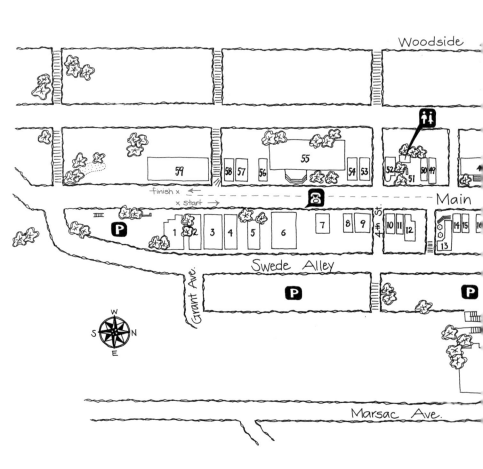

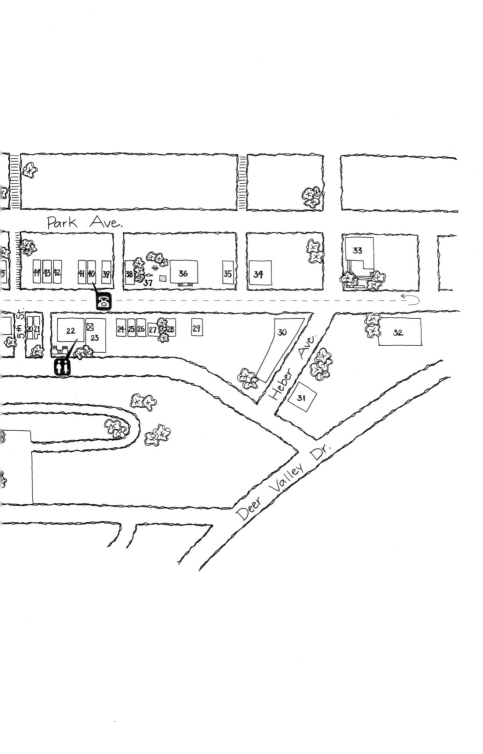

Park Ave.

is open daily from lunch on. The building's metal cornice and globe centerpiece recall popular Victorian architectural motifs.

Park City was once an alcohol oasis, its saloons second only to mines in number and prominence. Since a worker's quarters were usually cramped by large families or boarders, social life played out in public houses where people found comradeship and sociability. In the 1890s the city council passed a Sunday closing ordinance to prevent drinking on the Sabbath, although Jewish tavern owner Amos Mosher kept his open until a court forced compliance.

The parking lot above the Wasatch Brew Pub is the former site of a long row of saloons. William Donovan, Gus Carlson, and brothers Peter and Joseph Butkavitch all ran pre-Prohibition bars there. After Prohibition saloons operated as pool halls or drugstores and dispensed "medicinal" booze and narcotics.

In 1921 the upper Main Street pool halls were closed in response to a grass-roots action by Ma and Pa McGree. Underage brothers Tom and Frankie McGree picked a fight with a police officer on a drinking spree and landed in the dungeon below City Hall. When their parents found how easy it was to obtain liquor, they accused the police of taking pool hall payoffs.

A creek, now diverted underground, once ran past here. Originally it was known for its crystal clarity, but by the 1930s residents called Silver Creek "Poison Creek" because it carried mine tailings and city sewage.

Proceed north toward the bottom of Main Street. Notice through the gap between the Wasatch Brew Pub and Rasband Dance Hall the publicly-funded mural by Andrea Leichliter (completed in 1995) on the Swede Alley retaining wall. Also notice the red stone foundation to the old Rasband building.

2. Rasband Dance Hall (268 Main Street)

This two-story frame structure replaced Joe Dudler's brewery in 1900 after it was destroyed by fire. James Rasband, Park City's first Mormon bishop, converted the building into a dance hall in 1913. After World War I, when Park City mothers wanted to rent the hall to celebrate the soldiers' return, they were turned down because the enterprising owner wanted to organize his own dance for $150 in profits.

The Elks fraternal lodge later bought the hall. When they sold it to Dominic Giacoma who owned other properties on upper Main, they extracted a promise that it would not be used as a dance hall to compete with their own hall. Instead, Giacoma turned it into a hotel.

Much later cookie magnate Debbi Fields bought the building and started a candy factory with Rube Goldberg-esque machines purchased from Whitman's Chocolate Company. The upper floor was a dormitory for students of the Fields cookie college. The factory has since closed, but a Mrs. Fields logo remains. The current principal occupant of the building, the Morning Ray Cafe and Bakery, or "The Ray," is a favorite breakfast hangout for Parkites.

Continue north, past the Dudler Dorms, to the McPolin Bottle Works.

3. McPolin Bottle Works (306 Main Street)

Considered pretentious for its original plate glass windows when built, this building once housed the bottle works of Murty, Dan, and Larry McPolin, three brothers from South Dakota. The McPolins initially specialized in soda water but added adult favorites the following year, including wines, liquors, and cigars (while still catering to "family trade"). They also sold bottled libations. Owen Greenan, formerly of the Crescent Mine, was an investor in the venture.

With $1,000 the McPolins purchased for their bottle works the land and wreckage of Henry Freeman's American Hotel, ground zero for the Great Fire of 1898. By most accounts the fire started in the hotel kitchen and spread to surrounding buildings eventually consuming all but three downtown buildings. It was not the first major fire at the hotel. Another in the summer of 1885 took with it buildings to the north and south. With no gap between buildings, one can easily see why. Fortunately, all American Hotel owners were insured.

In one corner of the McPolin building was a barber shop and later a leather shop. Gus Carlson's saloon was situated here in 1909. Mike Yellowvich took over from Carlson and opened the Vienna Pool Room which the city closed in 1920 for being an Industrial Workers of the World (IWW) hangout. The IWW was a radical early twentieth-century labor union which, during the summer of 1919 when mine workers' wages were reduced from 75 cents to 50 cents a day due to alleged postwar surplus, encouraged miners to strike. The miners belonged for the most part to more conservative unions, but non-local IWW activists were the main impetus behind the strike and demanded a six-hour, $5.50 workday.

Mine owners browbeat the IWW-inspired miners, claiming in newspaper ads:

Which shall it be? The red flag or the glorious old red, white and blue? Patriotic citizens! Loyal Americans! Let us stand out and be counted. Show your colors! Unfurl old glory and let neighbors see where you stand on this issue. There is a mighty monster in the form of Bolshevism growing up in parts of the Old World that destroys Government, Individual Freedom, Home Life—everything that we hold dear. Let us see that it gets no foothold in our land.

Miners eventually capitulated, waiving compensation even for their two months' unemployment. Miners Hospital, which relied on deductions from wages, collapsed. When in February 1920 IWW activists tried once again to raise a strike, weary, angry miners took to the streets to drive them out of town. The Vienna Hall closed the next month.

John Davich purchased the building in 1936 and opened The Grill Bar. Davich was a Park City historian, archivist, and collector of antique telephone and saloon tokens. The building is now home to Cisero's Ristorante (open for lunch and dinner) and Nightclub (under the restaurant with a dance floor and two bars).

4. Giacoma Building (312 Main Street)

Dominic Giacoma, an Italian immigrant who owned several other properties on upper Main Street, built this two-story brick building in 1926 on the site of the Park City Meat Market grocery store and sausage factory, operated by Joseph Brandl and later James Rasband. Mark Prothro, the building's owner, renovated it beginning in the 1980s. The building now houses Nativo, a clothing and home-furnishings gallery, as well as the Rock and Silver Shop. Although flat, the brick façade has decorative key stones over upper-level windows and a soldier row of cornice bricks.

The new brick building which houses the Saguaro Gallery and Rocky Mountain Chocolate Factory next door was built in 1990 on the former site of the Fisher Brewing Company offices which rented space to the White Front Pool Hall during Prohibition. Though of recent construction, the building's design reflects the influence of the Giacoma Building. Next door, with the wooden portico and false balcony, is the McLeod Building.

5. Mary McLeod Building (320 Main Street)

When Mary McLeod built this one-story frame structure next to the Dewey Theater after the 1898 fire, the local paper gratefully observed, "One by one the gaps are being filled." The space was rented to a confectionery but eventually sold to the James Sullivan family for the Star Club and Park Tavern. The lively series of wooden arches and dentils creates a pleasing façade.

Red Banjo Pizzeria was opened here by Pete Toly in 1963, anticipating Park City's transformation into a resort town. Continue north past the Vie "European Spa" building to the Egyptian Theater.

6. Egyptian Theater (328 Main Street)

The town's first theater, the Grand Opera House, was built a few steps down the street where the old Golden Rule Building sits today. Residents found the hall inadequate for theatrical presentations, and when it burned down in 1898, mine owners John Judge and David Keith built the Dewey Theater here where their Main Street stables had been. Occupying a space 46 feet by 116 feet, the Dewey seated 600 on hardwood opera chairs and featured a sixteen-foot-high arched ceiling. The floor pivoted and could be sloped toward the stage during shows and leveled for balls and receptions. Judge and Keith originally intended to lease an upper floor for Masonic lodge rooms, but Masons made other plans and a second story never materialized. Architect S. C. Sherrill, who built Keith's First National Bank building where the Silver Queen Hotel now stands, designed the theater. It was named after George Dewey, hero of the recent Spanish-American War. Besides plays and dancing, when bowling became a fad, a ten-pin alley was constructed in the basement.

The theater's opening spectacular, "On the Swanee River," was noted for its inclusion of "colored" actors. The audience was informed that the plot did not "depend upon them to attract attention," "introduced them to display the perfectly natural songs, dances, and pastimes of plantation hands," and assured that "when the scene is finished the darkies were no more in evidence."

The next year the theater was the scene of an ugly, if more amusing, political spectacle. An Indian hypnotist conjured up William Jennings Bryan, the "free-silver" Democratic presidential candidate who opposed the gold standard that devalued silver. When Republicans hissed, the show erupted into a free-for-all. Despite the brawl, Parkites were later seen on the streets mimicking the mesmerizer's techniques. More controversy surfaced the next year when a burlesque show scandalized some locals. Eventually the theater was converted into a silent movie house.

In 1916 the Dewey collapsed under heavy snow. Before it did, the manager realized that the building was caving in and, fearing a stampede, told the projectionist to play the movie faster than normal while he braced the attic's sagging beams. The implosion occurred shortly after the audience left.

John Rugar built the Egyptian Theater ten years later, designed in the 1920s Egyptian Revival style, an architectural companion to Utah's Perry Theater in Ogden, both influenced by Warner's Egyptian Theater in Los Angeles. Seattle mystic C. R. Berg was brought to Park City to direct placement of faux-Egyptian-artifact decorations. Vaudevilles played here, and later the theater showed the town's first "talkies."

The theater became the LuAnn when it changed hands in the 1940s, and the Silver Wheel when it was sold again and remodeled in 1963. At that time it showcased old-fashioned melodramas. When the theater was sold again in 1973, it continued to stage melodramas but added more contemporary movie screenings.

Community boosters Randy and Debbi Fields (of Mrs. Fields Cookies) purchased the Silver Wheel in 1981, renovated it, and rechristened it the Egyptian, resulting in the first major clash between the Fieldses and the Park City establishment. The Fieldses argued with the Historic Commission over whether their renovation followed closely enough the building's historic architecture. Later financial problems touching all areas of the Fieldses' interests led to possible foreclosure, and they were forced to sign the building over to the Resolution Trust Corporation (RTC). In 1993, when RTC put the theater on the block, Parkites banded together to form the non-profit S.O.S. (Save Our Stage) and ensured its use as a community theater. The Egyptian continues to stage live drama and hosts independent movies at the annual Sundance Film Festival.

The new metal and cinderblock structure between the theater and the old Golden Rule building (Black Pearl) is on the site of Dan Haran's famous Center Saloon. Police raided Haran's pool hall regularly during Prohibition, suspecting a bootlegging "combine." His license was denied in 1921. The building remained vacant until, ironically, Harry Derry and John Terry opened the city's first state-run liquor store here in 1937. After World War II the Miners' Union and Veterans of Foreign Wars used the building for meetings. It was demolished in March 1974.

7. Golden Rule Store (350 Main Street)

The Golden Rule building stands where once were the Opera House, Maple Dance Hall, and later American Theater. The street-front side was divided into two retail spaces with a hallway leading to the dance hall and theater behind. Though simple in design, notice the modillions running along the cornice line. The smaller southern portion of the building housed the Golden Rule, part of the retail chain that later adopted its owner's name, J. C. Penney. When the dance hall was destroyed by fire in 1909, the Golden Rule built the present building with a similar layout. With branches in Wyoming, Idaho, Utah, and Nevada, the Golden Rule was the strongest retail firm in the West in the 1910s. In 1934 the building became a drugstore, a grocery store through the 1970s, and then Scarpelli's Black Pearl, a popular nightclub.

Continue past Sgt. Leisure clothing store to the old Elvers Saloon with the wooden balcony, now Trouts Original Dry Goods and Fly Shop.

8. Elvers Saloon (354 Main Street)

John H. Elvers rebuilt his saloon here after the 1898 fire. Four years later he sold it to saloon owner Dan McPolin who was succeeded by Pat Clark and his Bank Saloon. The two-story frame gable-roofed building, with sandstone foundation, once featured a broad porch to the south where Sgt. Leisure is now located, connecting it to the Maple Dance Hall and boarding house (now the Black Pearl) run by fire chief Clarence Hays. The second story is a later addition, as are the surface façade decorations.

In 1909 Hays was irritated by noise rising from Clark's saloons and charged Clark with running a disorderly house, the euphemism for a brothel. When a police officer arrived, Clark accused the officer in colorful language of giving Mrs. Hays preferential favors. The city council revoked Clark's license.

In 1989 the Elvers Saloon building—having since housed the Old Hat Store and later Cowboys and Indians western design store—was considered an eyesore. Jerry Gilomen, who purchased the building that year, enlisted help from Salt Lake City architect Louis Ulrich to completely renovate it. Discovery of charred walls led renovators to suspect that the building had survived the 1898 fire. But contemporary newspaper reports identify only three survivors: the Marsac Mill, the McLaughlin Office Building, and the saved-though-gutted City Hall.

In the late 1970s when the saloon was being renovated, workmen dug beneath two false floors to discover a prohibition-era tunnel, stocked with sixty whiskey bottles, which had extended under Main Street to where the Eating Establishment now stands.

Continue north past the patio of the Barking Frog Grill to the old Frankel Clothing Store. Notice the original brickwork and sandstone quoins and molding.

9. Julius Frankel Clothing Store (368 Main Street)

In the 1880s Park City's first library stood here. The lot remained unimproved for ten years after the 1898 fire until, in 1907, Julius Frankel moved his clothing store to this location. Born in Germany in 1868, he was brought to the United States by his uncle, Park City mercantilist Samuel Ascheim, in 1885. Frankel worked at his uncle's store and at the Ontario mine until he opened his own store in 1896 at several Main Street sites before and after the Great Fire. An orthodox Jew, Frankel confused unaware neighbors by closing on Jewish holidays. He later retired to Southern California and died there in 1957. In the 1920s James and Sarah Farrell ran a boarding house for immigrant and native miners, and the building was subsequently renovated in 1966 as the Silver Palace Saloon. In honor of those boarding housekeepers who expanded their real estate holdings, Swede Alley once carried the Farrell name.

In the 1970s Mount Air Variety Store was here, and then a restaurant. In 1977 Sunn Classic Pictures renovated the building as one of their Main Street headquarters. Sunn Classic produced the 1970s television series "Life and Times of Grizzly Adams" and the controversial feature-length film *In Search of Noah's Ark*. The production company moved the following year into the Masons' building. Later remodelings took place in 1983 and 1988. The current occupant, the Barking Frog restaurant (open daily for dinner), boasts a southwestern theme with wild game dishes.

The patio area once served the Senate Restaurant, a Chinese cafe, Utah's first 24-hour bistro. Turn-of-the-century youth met here on the edge of Chinatown after an evening of theater or dance.

Cross Fourth Street alley to the site of the old Corner Saloon.

10. Corner Saloon (402 Main Street)

"Are You Dry?" asked Mike Fitzpatrick's turn-of-the-century ads. Fitzpatrick and partners rebuilt their saloon here in the weeks following the 1898 fire and billed themselves as Park City's foremost "mixologists." Stiff competition ruled among saloon keepers who had to be good storytellers and genial men-of-the-people. Sometimes saloon keepers also added an exclusive club room where valued customers relaxed away from the riffraff, read current periodicals, conducted business, and indulged in liquid refreshments. Saloons, though rampant, were the most precarious business in the transient community.

The building's southern half, added in 1907, housed a saloon opened by Irishman Daniel Haran who also ran the Center Saloon up the street with partner Daniel Clark. Foster N. Salisbury's Corner Saloon operated from 1910 until Edwin D. Hurlburt followed in the saloon-to-soft-drink-parlor trend. He began here as a druggist in 1915 after moving with his family from Wyoming as a young man in 1900. At Hurlburt's one could enjoy a Golden Orangeade for 5 cents or more potent concoctions until he was caught masking alcohol as medicine. He argued that if he were guilty, so was every druggist in the state. Hurlburt moved to Santa Barbara, California, in 1918 and opened a hotel.

Hurlburt's gave way to the Miners' Find saloon operated by the Putnam family, and later the Consumer's Cooperative store from 1937-42. In 1972 Bill Coleman and Dick Miller opened Solid Muldoon's, named after an early twentieth-century miner. The co-op specialized in après-ski aperitifs and entertainment.

Next door is the old Wilson Building, now Mountain Tops clothing store.

11. Wilson Building (408 Main Street)

Charles M. Wilson located his doctor's office here both before and after the 1898 fire, although Barney Riley and Patrick Towey, Irish immigrants and old-time Park City saloon keepers, adapted the building to their own needs in 1900. In addition to saloons, Towey ran a livery stable on upper Main in the 1880s. After Riley's death in 1917 the city opened a public gymnasium here, and the building was later purchased by the Athenaeum Women's Society. The Athenaeum, one of the Park's longest existing social institutions, was organized in 1897 as a social welfare organization.

The L-shaped wooden structure with the shingled bay next door is the old St. Louis Bakery.

12. St. Louis Bakery (412 Main Street)

August Fuelling was a Bavarian general who was demoted to captain for marrying a circus performer. Disgruntled, he immigrated to

America, fought in the Civil War to gain U.S. citizenship, and headed west to Utah. As a non-Mormon, he had trouble making a go of business in Salt Lake City, so he moved to Park City in 1881 and managed a bakery on the corner of Fifth Street and Main. Three years later, when he bought the business, he moved it here and called it the St. Louis Bakery in honor of his second wife's home town.

In April 1892 Fuelling was reading the newspaper in the bakery's backroom when his daughter Hope's dead body was brought in and placed before him. She had been walking near the tracks north of the Union Pacific Depot with her suitor Louis Paradise when a rival, Milton Trotman, fired on the couple. Paradise, assuming he was the target, fled, but Trotman shot Hope three times before turning the gun on himself. Trotman was Fuelling's brother-in-law.

The Fuelling family moved to Ogden after the tragedy but eventually returned to open a corner grocery on lower Park Avenue. Fuelling retired around 1915.

Albert Duerr and John F. Flanagan operated Fuelling's bakery after he left for Ogden. They rebuilt after the 1898 fire but later sold the building to George and William J. Huddy and moved the St. Louis Bakery across the street. In 1916 an oven fire in their 579 Main Street bakery spread to connecting businesses. The fire marshall condemned the building but the owners continued anyway. The Huddy Brothers operated here into the 1930s as the Park City Bakery.

In 1972 Otto Mileti renovated the building's façade and opened Mileti's Italian restaurant. Still here, Mileti's serves creative homemade pastas and has a bar upstairs.

Next door to the north, including Muskoka Lakes clothing store, is Cafe Terigo Plaza.

13. Cafe Terigo Plaza (418 and 424 Main Street)

This new brick plaza and complex of buildings sit on the former site of Bourne's Boarding House, one of the town's original hostelries. In 1882 a Mrs. Bourne advertised room and board for $13 a week, while her chef, a talented but short-tempered Chinese immigrant, became known for wielding a carving knife at a dissatisfied diner. Ellen Connor adopted the business around 1885 and marketed the house by providing open-air band concerts on the hotel's balcony. After the fire, on the 4th of July, Connor opened a new 16-room Queen Anne-style hotel called the Salt Lake House. Contemporary accounts called it the handsomest building on Main Street.

Just north of the hotel, about mid-plaza, was the *Park Record* building. The paper, founded in 1880 by James Shupbach and acquired in 1884 by Samuel Raddon, was an opinionated, colorful, anti-Chinese, anti-Mormon newspaper. The *Record* had just completed construction when it was destroyed by the 1898 fire and for a while was published from a tent. Then, from a new building on the same site, Raddon continued. Farther north, where Cafe Terigo now stands, Willis A.

Adams, who developed a lighting technique for underground pictures in mines, rebuilt his photography stand called The Studio. Patrons entered The Studio from the side of the building, while the front was leased to First National Bank. When the bank completed its own building, Adams and partner Charles Prisk filled the space with a stationery and notions business, targeting those who appreciated "dainty and novel home decorations," objets d'art, books, and sweets.

Adams donated space to the Women's Relief Committee which coordinated assistance for fire victims. Four women from each of the city's churches served on the committee, operating a donation depot, funneling outside assistance, directing relief distribution, and organizing sewing and mending circles.

North of The Studio was once site of Dr. Edward Le Compte's office. Le Compte, one of the street's most eminent and permanent residents, lived here four decades. He had fought with Custer and was a fan of Deer Valley's race-horse track.

Returning to existing structures, Cafe Terigo, open for lunch and dinner, is a favorite movie star haunt during the annual Sundance Film Festival. Next door, the squatty wooden structure now housing Park City Pizza Company and a tiny but convenient market downstairs, was where legendary Pop Jenks worked.

14. Jenks Photography and Confectionery (430 Main Street)

Joseph E. "Pop" Jenks, Jr., was a local fixture nicknamed "Mr. Park City." Ironically, the only reason he stayed in town was because he was too poor to leave.

Jenks was born in Kansas in 1886 and travelled with Wells Fargo Express, the railroads, and the military during the Spanish-American War. After the war Jenks journeyed through Colorado and Utah selling photographic services along the way. When his boss disappeared with his pay, Jenks made the best of his consignment to Park City.

Jenks lived at the Bogan Boarding House and worked at the Oak Saloon and the post office, developing negatives in his room at night. The building, which he purchased in 1919, had been Hurlburt's drugstore and Thomas Timlin's and George O'Neil's cigar store, re-built after the 1898 fire. O'Neil served as city treasurer and as agent for the Summit County branch of the Chatauqua Society, a New York-based group that promoted recreation for moral development.

The Depression forced Jenks out of photography and into confections. Eventually the cafe did well enough for Jenks to open Lower Pop Jenks' Cafe on Park Avenue, and he continued operating these after his wife's death in 1947. He also served in the Utah legislature as a stalwart Republican. Among his many accomplishments, he is credited with bringing skiing to Ecker Hill in 1924 in the Snyderville mountain area near the present-day Utah Winter Sports Park. Pop retired in 1970. Jim Park renovated Pop's to serve as the Carbide Lamp restaurant.

Upon Pop's death in 1971, Park City businesses closed their doors for the memorial services:

Death of Pop Jenks has created a void in Park City which cannot be filled. Men come and go, as they have come and gone through the ages, and nobody lives forever, but it seemed Pop Jenks would go on and on. . . . Jenks was always the same. Through half a dozen Park City depressions Pop predicted that Park City would rise again, and his warm smile, his firm handclasp, his words of friendship never varied through good times and bad. . . . He did not know the meaning of intolerance or resentment. Pop Jenks was the man all men wish they could become. "Be sure to give my love to Pop."

15. Rocky Mountain Bell Telephone (434 Main Street)

William P. Woodruff established a stationery and newsstand here in 1894 but was so devastated by the 1898 fire that he sold out to Charles Prisk who moved the salvaged stock to the store he shared with Willis Adams. The *Park Record* "deplored" Woodruff's "weak spirits."

Rocky Mountain Bell Telephone Company employed noted Utah architect Richard Kletting to design and build this two-story brick business block in September 1898. Kletting had previously designed the Utah State Capitol and other prominent Salt Lake City commercial and university buildings. Bell Telephone installed Park City wires in September 1881 with an exchange headquartered in the post office, then the Marsac Mill office. The lower floor of the new building contained an office, private talking booths, and supply rooms, while the upstairs had employee living apartments. In 1911 Mountain States Telephone and Telegraph Company bought and preserved operations in this building. It is now the Irish Camel Ltd., a Mexican restaurant open for lunch and dinner.

Passing the Quality Interiors and Gifts Building (436 Main Street), one of the most ornate façades on Main Street adorns the old Rogers Building. Remodeling in 1973-74 uncovered the exterior which had been painted over. Notice the lead-glass window transoms between upper-level pilasters.

16. Rogers Building (438 Main Street)

Margaretta V. Rogers hired Salt Lake architect Carl Neuhausen to design and oversee construction of this impressive 50-by-50-foot square building in April 1899. The pressed metal façade was obtained by mail order. Rogers sold the building to George Barton in 1901, who lost it to the bank three years later. By 1914 it was the John J. Fitzgerald Confectionery, and in the 1940s the Orange Blossom Confectionery. For many years the building housed Car 19 restaurant. After a fire ravaged the structure, the façade was all that could be saved. The building has been reconstructed with a wooden slat front and now houses the Szechwan Chinese Restaurant and the new Cozy bar downstairs with furnishings

Rogers Building , detail (I. 16)

from the original Cozy. Note the sign identifying your "First Chance" or "Last Chance" for a drink, depending on your direction.

17. Farrell Building (440 Main Street)

James Farrell, who owned considerable property in Chinatown and whose name was originally attached to Swede Alley, built this Victorian frame commercial building in 1900. Park City Variety, a candy and sporting goods store, later occupied the site. It is now Texas Red's barbecued ribs house, a family restaurant.

18. Andrew Furniture and Hardware (442 Main Street)

One of the town's "Cousin Jacks," a pejorative for Cornish nepotism, Frank A. Andrew emigrated to the states in 1871, to Park City in 1883, and mined for nine years before opening a hardware and furniture store in 1892. After the 1898 fire he rebuilt a 25-by-65-foot brick building with a sandstone foundation making it less vulnerable to fire. He died of miner's consumption, a lung infection caused by exposure to metallic dusts, thirty years after leaving mining.

The store housed John Cunningham & Sons Hardware in 1928, although ownership remained with Andrew's widow. In 1939 she sold to John and Olga Aimos for their City Cash Market, and in the 1970s occupants included a beauty shop and ice cream parlor. Now it is Christmas on Main Street, Alex's basement-level French restaurant (one of the city's best), and Old Town Gallery which features contemporary art by internationally-known artists.

19. Post Office (450 Main Street)

The Park City Bank emerged on this cornersite in 1880, built by David C. McLaughlin, partner to Edward P. Ferry in many of the city's original mining and real estate ventures. The bank provided systematic exchange in the rapidly growing town, as well as telegraphic transfers, foreign exchange, and the all-important buying and selling of ore and bullion. In December 1892 McLaughlin reported that the bank was in robust health and expected indefinite growth. The next year, in June 1893, patrons were shocked by the bank's closing. Its collapse corresponded to the national panic of 1893, one of the worst economic periods in American history. McLaughlin's company tried to reorganize to escape creditors, but this failed and the new company was forced into bankruptcy. This caused a run on First National Bank which was barely able to withstand the pressure. The Silver Queen Hotel is a replica of the Park City Bank.

Three other buildings, Peter McPherson's Dry Goods, the Hub Saloon, and Bettinger's office-lease building, also stood here adjacent to the bank. When German immigrant George Bettinger rebuilt after the

1898 fire, he decided to open a saloon, a 20-by-40-foot wood-frame, tin-roof building which would be the fifteenth post-fire saloon in town. Bettinger paid a $150 license for the "privilege of dispensing liquid damnation" before dying four months later at age sixty-two.

Congress appropriated funds as early as 1916 for a Park City Post Office, but residents ignored the matter until the *Park Record* warned against stalling. The stipulation that it be on a large corner lot caused problems because corner sites were rare and space requirements implied consolidation of several lots, all of which added up to more than the government was willing to spend. Residents accused one another of trying to influence site selection for selfish reasons. World War I postponed construction, and by the time the money was released, costs had escalated. Utah's senator Reed Smoot worked as liaison between federal and city officials to raise supplementary appropriations.

The government finally awarded a building contract and construction began in late 1920. While some boosted the project, others ridiculed the out-of-place "cookie-cutter" architecture and saucer-shaped roof that did not anticipate heavy snowfall, a detail the federal architect acknowledged he had overlooked.

In 1967 city fathers concluded that the pink-stuccoed building with classical lines did not fit the city's western boomtown focus and convinced U.S. General Services to hire Salt Lake City architect Burtch W. Beall to design a make-over in Park City Style. The office was again renovated and expanded in 1975, though it still has a flat roof.

Cross Fifth Street to the corner brick building, noticing the new City Hall location on the hill to your far right, originally the Marsac Elementary School.

20. Utah Power and Light Building (506 Main Street)

The old Marsac Mill Office, formerly at this address, was one of three Main Street commercial buildings to escape the 1898 fire, although three of its storehouses were lost. The mill itself sat behind Old City Hall astride Silver Creek and was built by Edward P. Ferry to process ore from one of the first working mines, the Flagstaff. The Marsac Company was incorporated in November 1881, with the mill ready by the end of winter. The company's holdings were transferred to the Daly Company in July 1885. Locals complained that the mill's sulfuric fumes seared the lungs, especially when the wind blew up-canyon. The building included rooms for general business, Ferry's private office, and a sleeping room.

Born in Grand Haven, Michigan, to Presbyterian missionaries among the Mackinac Indians, Ferry acquired sawmills and timber properties while in Michigan and, in 1878, came west to examine recently acquired mining properties. He led a band of investors dubbed the Michigan Bunch, including David C. McLaughlin and Frederick Nims. The developers were prone to throw their capital weight around and often came to loggerheads with old-timers.

One of the most notorious acts perpetrated by the Bunch was the townsite patent affair. Park City was originally cleared and surveyed by members of the McHenry Mining Company, with shafts in McHenry Canyon between Deer and Jordanelle valleys. As people moved in, businesses and residences were built wherever the ground seemed level enough. The federal government held title to all the property but put forward a variety of arrangements whereby private citizens and companies could develop or own federal land. Early settlers never bothered to explore these legal options either out of ignorance or because the camp's future was so tenuous.

In 1874 Nims applied for a patent to the townsite using Sioux scrip, land vouchers the government offered Minnesota Sioux to relocate away from midwestern settlers. Whether Nims had Sioux blood is doubtful, which perhaps explains why he later substituted another form of payment, vouchers from a Mexican property holder compensated after the Mexican-American War. Then Nims offered to sell or rent to Park City settlers the properties on which they already had homes or businesses. He transferred title to the townsite land to Ferry in 1880. At that time Park City was a town of 350 buildings and around 3,500 residents. Disgruntled old-timers took Nims and Ferry to court several times but never prevailed. They were all eventually forced to buy their homes back from Ferry's townsite company.

Ferry was a member of the Utah legislature, representing the non-Mormon Liberal Party, and in 1891 led the Trans-Mississippi Congress for western economic development. He died of a stroke in 1917 in a Los Angeles retirement home.

After Ferry's death the Marsac office property was used by the Park City Water Works until it was sold to Utah Power and Light in 1926. The Marsac Mill had boasted the city's first electric light in 1885. The new technology was not in general use until the turn of the century. The Park City Power Company was an accessory to Robert C. Chambers's Ontario mine plant on lower Park Avenue.

In 1926 the mill, which survived the fire, fell to Park City progress. Utah Power & Light's offices had been at the Alamo Building since after the 1898 fire, but it needed a new building more suited to modern needs. Salt Lake City architects Carl Scott and George Welch designed the new building. They also designed the Marsac School. The first floor originally contained offices, salesrooms (where the latest electrical home gadgetry was displayed), and service department workrooms. The second floor housed the company's division manager and family. It is still used by UP&L. Its simple, institutional design is more formal than other Main Street buildings. Notice the hand-carved wood sign.

Next door, with the lavender scrolled braces and window trim, is Dolly's Books.

21. Dolly's Books (510 Main Street)

The last remaining intact pre-1898 Main Street building stood here until it too burned down in 1992. The "fire-proof" building which became Dolly's Books before the fire was originally David McLaughlin's law and mining offices. McLaughlin was one of the Michigan Bunch and managed Edward Ferry's Anchor Mining Company. Trained in law at the University of Michigan, McLaughlin was principal in the ill-fated Park City Bank venture. He was also Utah's first non-Mormon state legislator. He died suddenly at the age of forty-six in 1901.

After McLaughlin's death the building was used alternately as a residence and a doctor's office. John Sharp remodeled and fancified the simple façade in 1970 for an art gallery, studio, and residence. In 1979 Dolly Makoff moved her bookstore here from the Richardson Mortuary building down the street. When Makoff left the business to start the successful Writers at Work Conference, which hosts national literary talent annually in Park City, Los Angeles transplants Norman and Claire Weiss acquired the store, joined by their son Gary.

In August 1992, following a day of Arts Festival revelry, the building caught fire. Arson was suspected as retribution for Summit County planning commissioner Gary Weiss's criticism of the Town Lift (later Summit Watch) Development on lower Main Street. The Weisses were also embroiled with neighbors over construction of a guest house. Police, however, soon discounted the arson theory.

Shortly after the fire the Weisses issued an unusually emotional statement to the local press. It reveals much about the city's ambivalence about the past and rapid development:

We say the town has changed . . . and each day as we take the measure of the tempests in this beautiful teapot, we number the things that aren't the same. The things that aren't as good. The things we wish were still. . . . And so we count "units," and dogs and visitor nights, acre feet, miles of trails, heights on Main Street, historic this and development that, and . . . . [d]evelopers come from everywhere. Sagebrush hills become green foam rubber lawns. Mail delivery becomes a Human Right. Things come. Things go. Today I really don't know if Dolly's will be back. But I know we'll be here. I know we'll be in it: bitching and moaning and trying. Failing often, but thanking God we were here now and when the best of humans were here with us and chose to be our friends.

The Weisses rebuilt. Overcoming their ambivalence to change and city politics, they fought for 800 additional square feet for expansion in exchange for affordable housing above the store and improvement of the walkway between Main Street and Swede Alley. The new building's design is that elusive yet ubiquitous Park City Style.

Just past the little brick walkway and ticket-reservation booth, beyond basement-level Main Street Liquor Store, is the old brick Diem Saddlery.

22. John Diem's Saddlery and Harness Shop (518 Main Street)

After being burned out in the 1898 fire, John Diem, who managed to save most of his stock, re-built this brick building and quickly restarted business. Coming from a harness shop in Payson, Utah, he had begun here three years previously. After a setback with a dishonest partner, Diem eventually grew to become a leading merchant and owner of several mining properties.

The building was later a furniture store, then the town's library in 1910, which was funded by a referendum in which a total of fifty votes were cast. The librarian, who constantly complained of the cold, thought the building inadequate. Books were moved to the Miners Hospital in 1982 and now reside in the old high school on Park Avenue. Wyoming Woolens, a contemporary western-wear clothing store, is located here.

Next door is the Old City Hall and whistle tower. Notice the stone window sills.

23. Old City Hall (528 Main Street)

The original two-story city hall was built on this site in the winter of 1885-86. The building housed courts, police, city recorder, marshall, and fire department, as well as the telephone company. The downstairs contained "apartments to protect the drunkard from winter blasts and the evil-doer from harm"—in other words, the jail. In 1891 workers installed iron stay bars in the walls to prevent the building from bowing and replaced the roof. Only the hall's brick walls remained after the 1898 fire, but a new city hall was ready for re-occupation the following winter. The renovated brick Victorian structure has ornamental arches over three main entrances. The southernmost arch covered a garage door for the fire department's hose cart. The three second-story windows are flanked with pilasters.

Shortly after reconstruction, a wood fire alarm tower was added to the south. In January 1887 the city council enacted a curfew law which required boys under sixteen to be home by 8:00, later changed to 10:00 p.m. The 1,500-pound bell was replaced in 1905 by an electronic siren which continued to sound a "Ten O'Clock Whistle" for curfew. In 1980, when the siren's circuitry failed, a councilwoman suggested it was because Parkites had stopped attending to their heritage. The tower was restored in 1983-84 as part of the City Hall restoration but no longer employs the siren. Salt Lake City's Cooper/Roberts Architects designed the restoration.

City Hall houses the Park City Museum of History and Territorial Jail as well as the town's historical society offices. The displays are re-creations of mine shafts which hardly convey the dank, foul pits they actually were. The dungeon—the real thing—still has a Wobblies slogan burned on one of the cell walls. The *Park Record* for the period, which gives detailed court reports, lists the arrest of only one IWW activist, George E. Colton, an organizer from the Bingham copper mining camp. Colton visited early in 1920 to raise a strike. While he was handing out handbills on Main Street, a fight with a local miner developed. Police held him on a vagrancy charge knowing he could not make the $50

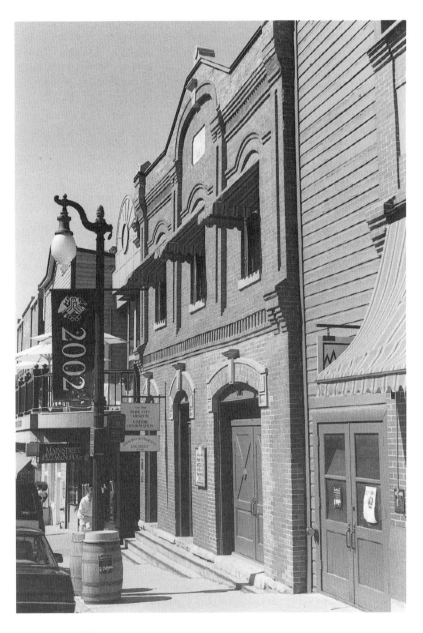

Old City Hall (I. 23)

Old City Hall , detail (I. 23)

bond. Besides accommodations for labor activists, city hall provided space for community and religious organizations. The Christian Scientists met here for many years. Public restrooms are located to your right down the brick walkway following this building.

Proceed past the tin- and glass-fronted Main Street Pizza and Noodle house (530 Main Street) to the old Masonic Hall, now the Great Garb clothing store and entrance to the popular Riverhorse Cafe (above the Pizza and Noodle House), which offers contemporary dinner cuisine.

24. Masonic Hall (540 Main Street)

This ground remained vacant for ten years after the 1898 fire until Masons built in 1908. Fraternal organizations such as the Freemasons were vital to the social fabric of nineteenth-century Utah communities, especially for non-Mormons who were denied the benefits of Utah's largest social institution. The lodge was first organized in June 1878 (chartered in 1880 as Uintah Lodge No. 7) and met originally at the Ontario School. Between 1883-98 members met in the opulently decorated second-story lodge room above Ascheim's Mercantile.

After the 1898 fire Masons performed ceremonies on Masonic Hill just east of here, north of Rossie Hill. Masonic rules allowed outdoor rites when lodges were unavailable, provided they took place "on one of the highest hills as did their ancient brethren." A special train brought visitors from Salt Lake City. The gathering was similar to one in Virginia City, Nevada, after a fire destroyed their lodge in 1876. The Park City event was said to have surpassed Nevada's because it took place 1,000 feet higher. The Sutton Brothers, merchants and Masons, leased the second-story of their post-fire building to the lodge soon after the historic conclave.

In 1908 the Masons' own two-story hall with basement, "grand in its simplicity," was erected by Ellsworth J. Beggs for $6,000. The diamond-shaped openings flanking the central window represent the juxtaposition of Masonry's two predominant symbols—the compass and square—combined into a diamond shape. In the 1970s the building was purchased by Sunn Classic Pictures, and in 1983 was restored to its original condition using old photographs by an interior design firm, Design Coalition.

Continue north.

25. Elks Lodge Building (550 Main Street)

This three-story concrete lodge hall was not constructed until 1922 for the Benevolent Protective Order of Elks No. 734. Previously the Elks met at the Old Social Hall and at Rasband's Hall. The B.P.O.E. was one of the last fraternal organizations established in Park City, and members still use the upper level for meetings, while the ground level is used for commercial purposes.

Continue north.

26. Squires Carpenter Shop (556 Main Street)

Richard E. Squires operated a carpenter's shop on the opposite side of Main Street before the fire and then relocated here around 1910. The building became John J. Murphy's barber shop in 1933 and now houses Images of Nature Gallery.

Proceed next door.

27. The Annex Rooming House (558 Main Street)

Atypically set back from the street, this substantial four-square plan frame building with hipped roof was first an office and then Lucy Penney's Annex Rooming House in 1907. Lydia Stanley and Henry Birkumshaw later became the building's proprietors. The name was changed to The Bucket which operated at various times as a saloon and rooming house.

Tom Mathews, a founding member of the Peace Corps and former *Salt Lake Tribune* Sunday editor, bought The Bucket when it was still a saloon in 1963. An alcoholic, he drank the greater share of his wares. The next year he entered and successfully completed treatment and went on to become the public relations director for the Lincoln Performing Arts Center in Manhattan, press secretary for Robert Kennedy's presidential campaign, and eventually president of Common Cause, the populist lobbying group. The building is now Silver Junction Mercantile, an antique gallery. Next door is the simple wooden structure that was once the Raddon Dye Works.

28. Raddon Dye Works (562 Main Street)

William J. Raddon built this sewing machine shop and dye works on the site of his old residence after the 1898 fire. He was the local Singer sewing machine agent. His wife and later daughter Alvina continued the business into the 1940s. The building has since been occupied by Purple Mushroom art shop, Miscellania giftstore, and now North Woods USA and Old Time Photo, two souvenir shops.

Continue next door. Although Old Town does not have a Burger King or Wendy's, it has Burgie's (570 Main Street) where you can get anything from a cheeseburger to a lambburger. Notice the distinctive blue wood framing and arched center top.

Continue past the Galleria Mall, which was constructed as the Grand Hotel Galleria in the mid-1980s and designed by architect John D. Carbine to complement the Park Hotel, to the old Feeney Building, now Ichiban Sushi restaurant and fish market.

29. Feeney Building (588 Main Street)

William Fennemore was one of the Park's most enterprising merchants. He built his first shop here in the late 1870s and expanded it several times, rebuilding the current two-story shop after the 1898 fire. He sold everything from produce to fireworks. The back of his building (called "The Mortuary") was reserved for undertaking. "Feeney" hung a small casket out front as his marquee, and old-timers remembered the way it would sway in the wind "moaning and groaning and making unearthly noises reminding one of departed spirits." One night the coffin mysteriously disappeared.

Jacob F. and William D. Richardson took over Feeney's mortuary business after the 1898 fire. The new structure was still known as the Feeney building. In addition to being a mortician, William was city marshall for a year. The Richardsons shared the building with the Salvation Army and George Ketchum's Bon Ton Barber Shop. In 1921 George M. Archer took over the mortuary and ran it along with a hearse-driven bootlegging operation through the 1940s. The Joseph Olpin Mortuary operated here before the building was readapted for retail space in the late 1960s.

Proceed north to the corner. You will pass the Repartee Gallery (592 Main Street) which features prominent regional artists, pass two wooden buildings with distinctive upper and lower bays, walk under the porticos of two boutique malls (Main Street Shops and 614 Main Street), and continue along the west wall of the imposing Silver Queen Hotel.

30. Silver Queen Hotel (632 Main Street)

The impressive Silver Queen was designed to recall the façade of the Park City Bank which defaulted in 1893. This exclusive condominium hotel boasts twelve spacious one- and two-bedroom suites. Reservations are required at least two to three months in advance.

Before the 1898 fire this site housed, among other buildings, the Parlor restaurant, the "Delmonico" of Park City, according to the *Record*. After the fire the site was occupied by Jim Lee Cafe and later by First and Last Chance Saloon.

The saloon became The Cozy under Hugh Steel, with Fonce Martinez as manager from 1928 to 1967, at which time Martinez took over exclusively. Steel was a former Union Pacific conductor, a hard-drinking gambling man whose clientele was drawn from the mines. The Cozy bootlegged throughout Prohibition, while Martinez alternated between bartending and mining and helping Steel run the card tables and slot machines. The Cozy's marquee read "Last Chance" from down the hill and "First Chance" coming up the hill, as does the new Cozy marquee up the street.

Martinez's son Rich, who became a city councilor, decided with his father to demolish the bar in 1979 to make room for other developments, including the Silver Queen established in 1982.

Cross Heber Avenue to continue north along lower Main Street. The White Pine Touring building to your right (on Heber Avenue) was the location of the Utah Coal and Supply Company offices.

31. Utah Coal and Supply Company (201 Heber Avenue)

From Park City's earliest days, this corner yard housed offices for the Utah Coal and Supply Company and railroad depot. Mining and real estate denuded the surrounding hillsides of timber shortly after the community was founded, so the coal company doubled as a lumber yard. Park City's mid-twentieth-century depression forced the company to close.

Continuing north on lower Main Street, following the rock wall, notice The Grille at the Depot to your right, which offers California cuisine and regional products such as pheasant lasagna, veal ravioli, and venison with cranberry-kumquat chutney. This lot also boasts a hand-made furniture studio. Heber Avenue used to run diagonally from Main Street north of the Utah Coal building but was later realigned to pass in front of the Silver Queen Hotel.

Past The Grille is the massive new Summit Watch development which occupies most of lower Main Street. You can see the chair lift across the street to the northwest. Notice how the modern cement, brick façade, sprayed-on stucco, and pressed-wood construction of these new buildings differ from nineteenth-century structures while attempting to recreate a post-modern play on historic styles.

32. Summit Watch Development (Lower Main Street)

Main Street used to terminate at the depot. Now it enjoys a three-block extension and will eventually intersect with Deer Valley Drive to the east. The Park City Depot grounds passed into the hands of Blaine Huntsman, Jr., and Ladd E. Christensen in 1982, who convinced the city to pursue plans envisioned by Trolley Square developers who had transformed a downtown Salt Lake City block into a popular shopping and dining mall. Huntsman and Christensen agreed to give up easement rights which now form part of Deer Valley Drive in exchange for development incentives including a waiver on height restrictions. Although the grade runs down hill, developers were not constrained to measure height from downhill troughs but from the highest point on the east side along Deer Valley Drive. The city also rezoned the area from Historic Resort to Historic Commercial to relieve density restrictions.

During the next several years development fell to different companies and finally to co-developers Moutainlands and the Marriott Corporation. Marriott's Summit Watch time-share condominiums will eventually encompass eight separate buildings, some of which will face Main Street, others Deer Valley Drive. Buildings on Main Street will have historic commercial façades; those on Deer Valley Drive will feature contemporized mining architecture. Parking will be underground, commercial businesses on the ground level, and living quarters above. A walkway over Main Street will move visitors from their condominiums to the ski lift. Streetlamps similar to those on Old Main Street were provided to establish some continuity.

Other plans include a new ski lift and a skier bridge over Woodside Avenue, with the possible realignment of Park Avenue to close it off at Ninth Street. Neighbors have objected, the planning commission has waffled, and developers have threatened to sue. In a compromise, the council lowered its eight-story height allowance to six stories—still two stories more than the standard zoning restriction—and provided $700,000 to improve streets, money from city redevelopment funds previously earmarked for schools and the fire department. Cooper/Roberts Architects, Park City restorationists, designed several of the development's modernized Victorian-style buildings.

This ends the first half of the tour. Cross over to the west side of Main Street and turn left. Proceed up Main Street (south) to the corner of Heber Avenue where a tile mural by Park City artist Lark Lucas stands. To your right, between Main Street and Park Avenue, is the Kimball Art Center, the largest gallery in Park City, representing both contemporary and traditional western art. It occupies what used to be the Kimball Garage.

33. Kimball Garage (638 Park Avenue)

On 4 July 1872 George Gideon ("Judge") Snyder and wife Rhoda ("Aunt Rhoda") raised a home-stitched American flag where Heber and Park avenues now intersect and announced the founding of Park City, a name the Snyders thought appropriate considering the lush wooded surroundings. Previously the area was known as Upper Parley's Canyon or Upper Kimball Junction, leading to the hybrid popular designation of Parley's Park, but ultimately Park City stuck. The Snyders built a two-room rectangular house here and later expanded it into a popular boarding house with horse and carriage stables.

In 1879, during a time when Mormons were excluded from federal offices, Snyder became a probate judge after renouncing his religion. Always a backslider, he had followed his Mormon parents to Utah in 1850 but continued on to California. Returning in 1857, he moved to the mountains to escape "King Brigham."

Snyder played a role in every aspect of Park City's founding. He established a ranch in what would become Snyderville, prospected the foothills, and founded the first passenger and freight express between here and Salt Lake City. He shipped the city's first ore, which he excavated from his "Green Monster Claim," later part of the Crescent Mining Company's holdings. His son Kimball maintained the stagecoach line even after the railroad arrived. Passengers were not "too shook up," Kimball said, when he raced the train up the mountain or competed with James Roach's Stages. A particularly nasty accident at Parley's Summit was blamed on a Roach driver's intentional swerve. Roach also managed The Oak tavern for forty-five years.

Two years after Snyder's death in 1887, Kimball Snyder sold the family stables to John Dexter & Sons Livery. Then in 1927 the owner of the Coal Team Barn, a Kimball by surname, bought the Dexter Livery. Burton Kimball had decided to switch from horses to automobiles and so constructed the Kimball Garage here, later modified by Eley Motors. William Kimball (no relation) renovated in 1972 for the art center, covering the brick garage with horizontal wood siding.

Cross Heber Avenue to the south. At this corner grocery merchant William D. Sutton established the Park Garage in 1919, the town's first automobile dealership. He sold Ford Runabouts and Touring Sedans for $550 to $825.

When the Lincoln Highway was created in 1915, automobile travel came into vogue in rural areas. The Lincoln Highway was a patchwork of local roads that at first amounted to nothing more than the placement of red-white-and-blue road markers. But as the highway was upgraded through Wasatch County, and as feeder routes were connected, the Parley's Canyon line of the Denver and Rio Grande Railroad declined in the face of competition and was finally discontinued in 1946. The Union Pacific line closed in 1977.

Walk south on Main Street. The building on your right is the more recent Fashion Coalition Building (613 Main Street) with shops on the lower level and offices upstairs. It is followed by the New Park Hotel.

34. New Park Hotel (605 Main Street)

James and Edward Berry were blacksmiths in a different building located at this address from at least 1891 until the late 1920s. Edward died in 1971 at the age of 89, the city's oldest native at the time. He was a familiar fixture on City Hall steps, where he spent his days reminiscing with friends along with his dog Lucky.

During the early years the Berry brothers employed Robert Wid-dison, a notorious drunkard who committed suicide in the smithy's woodshed. He left a note blaming his wife's religion: "Today is the last day alive on this earth. I have had Christian Science every time I have been home three times a day for the last ten or eleven years and I am tired and disgusted with it. I would rather be dead." Some neighbors sided with his long-suffering wife, others thought she was to blame.

The original Park Hotel was built in 1913, the present building around 1980. Continue south up Main Street to the Family Jewels gallery, formerly the Resort Saloon.

35. The Resort Saloon (591 Main Street)

One of the longer running bars in town, the Resort Saloon was first operated by George Wanning, born in 1859, who resided for a time at the original Park Hotel a few doors up the street. Henry J. Conlon retained the saloon's name when he acquired it around 1900, followed eight years later by George Matlovich and George Bielich, Austrian partners who were soon arrested for running a disorderly house. The case was dropped, but the *Park Record* continued to complain about "iniquitous proceedings" at the saloon. Prostitution was not limited to The Row on Heber Avenue, the best-known red-light district in town. Nor was the Resort the only Main Street saloon fronting for sex. While the shenanigans continued downstairs, the second floor was used by the Park City Boys Club, managed by future city marshall Ed Tracy.

In the 1920s the saloon became Sam De Angelo's Gold Label Club Room, then a dry cleaners in the 1950s around the time the second story burned. The ground level continued to be occupied, complete with a stairway leading nowhere, until it was renovated in 1972. It is now a jewelry store and White Wolf Gallery, with apartments upstairs.

Continue south past the small parking lot on your right to the Old Park Hotel, a large brick structure with a narrow, three-story wooden addition. No longer a hotel, the building houses a restaurant, club, and offices upstairs. Notice the decorative brickwork, the balcony with Egyptian columns, and fan-shaped lintels over the upper windows.

36. Old Park Hotel (573 Main Street)

Not to be confused with its newer namesake down the street, the original three-story Park Hotel was built here around 1880. The town's largest hotel, it included a spacious dining room, bar, parlor, and boasted a New York-trained French pastry chef. Henry Gray, the hotel's proprietor, skipped town in 1887 after squandering hotel funds on gambling debts. Gray was apprehended at Echo, Utah, and brought back to face angry creditors and disappointed guests. But the hotel flourished the next year when new management added more rooms in a "cottage" on the south side which spanned the block between Main Street and Park Avenue. Madame Mizpah, a celebrated clairvoyant, was among the hotel's prominent guests.

The hotel was re-built after the 1898 fire by George Hall and featured forty-two rooms, a dining room, parlors, and "sample rooms" where traveling salesmen set up temporary shops similar to today's trade shows. Daily rates ranged from $1.50 to $2.00. When the hotel burned again in 1912, it was re-built of brick the next year at a cost of $22,455. The basement level was leased to a paint store and to Maggie Bowman, a prominent early businesswoman who ran a millinery training school and employed young women to make hats.

In 1966 Vaughan Johnson acquired the property and inaugurated a $300,000 restoration. Bob and Jay Jones added heated waterbeds and the

Old Park Hotel, detail (I. 36)

Claimjumper restaurant in 1971. In 1978 new owners Lloyd Stevens and Provo car dealer Richard Ringwood launched an ambitious $2 million renovation, doubling the building's Main Street frontage. The hotel eventually engulfed a large square on the corner of what was Sixth Avenue and swallowed up what had been Hofstein's butcher shop and the old Summit County Mercantile, a Judge Mining Company store. The store opened in 1920, and miners' wages were paid in part with coupon booklets redeemable at the store, a gimmick neither they nor other merchants appreciated. The store closed in 1933.

The Claimjumper restaurant, open for dinner, has a western theme with entrees such as buffalo and Utah trout. The basement-level Down Under bar has live music.

Proceed a few steps up Main Street to Centennial Park.

37. Centennial Park (551 Main Street)

This small park with the "Sonata #9" sculpture by William J. Kranstover is where the International Order of Odd Fellows built after the 1898 fire. Financing came from charter member Thomas Cupit who made his fortune building the Ontario Mill. The second floor contained the lodge room, and the first floor was rented to Charles Murphy's saloon and Pete Durante's Main Hardware store. Durante's son Art, who met his father for the first time just before his father's death, moved west and took over the business. During the hard 1940s-50s when so many people wanted to move out, Durante made ends meet by starting a moving business. Older Parkites who remember him call this Art's Park.

Enter the park and look north to the wall of the Old Park Hotel. The painting of the cowboy and prostitute is by David Chaplin, a former Park City High School art teacher. Also note the flame memorial to promote Utah's forthcoming International Winter Olympics in the year 2002.

The next building south was originally the McNaughton Barber Shop.

38. McNaughton Barber Shop (541 Main Street)

Built around 1910, this two-story frame rectangular house provided space for a barber shop on the first floor and Art Messner's Mint saloon on the upper level through the 1940s. The building was remodeled in the 1970s with aluminum siding but was later restored to the original wood. During restoration architects discovered that the floor joists were leveled on liquor bottles and chunks of brick.

Now Hay Charlie, be sure to check out the "hats, boots, and dude's apparel" on the second level, including sterling silver belt buckles, leather boots, and felt hats from $150 to $1,200 depending on the beaver-pelt content.

McNaughton Barber Shop (I. 38)

Next door, past a narrow driveway, is the three-story Kimball Building with an impressive cut-glass fanlight over the entrance.

39. Kimball Building (537 Main Street)

Robert F. and Lawrence P. Kimball Brothers' Feed Stable once occupied this entire block. The Kimballs were original settlers and operated a stage line beginning in the 1870s. On the burnt-out site of the stables they constructed a new building to lease retail space.

Later Herbert W. "Bert" Deighton acquired the building for his Meat and Grocery Market. He began with a tin and hardware store in 1886 at the head of Main Street and later expanded into the food business at this location. The market's storefront began to dwindle in the 1920s when Deighton began subdividing, renting first to Greek partners Peter Farthelos and Tony Polychronis and then to John J. Ryan's shoe repair. When the building partially collapsed in 1966, its walls were rebuilt of concrete block. In 1977 Sunn Classic Pictures leased the building and remodeled its façade. The many-paned windows are out of character for the period.

Next door was the site of the Bates & Kimball Drug Store. Ownership remained in the Kimball family until 1939 as Ed Hurlburt's Park Pharmacy, Laurence B. Kimball's Park Floral, and the Silver Palace Confectionery. It was sold to former city attorney Louis B. Wight.

The one-story cinderblock building with a two-story wooden façade, now housing Main Street Deli, with sandwiches and drinks to stay or go, was originally a dentist's office.

40. Platt Dentist Office (525 Main Street)

Samuel W. Platt resided here with his wife Cordelia. After the 1898 fire the new building included Sam's office, a parlor, and "comfortable house-keeping apartments" which were what we know today as studio apartments. Platt was succeeded in 1920 by George Sheen, also a dentist. A concrete building replaced the old frame one in 1971, but the façade was redesigned by Salt Lake City architect Allen Roberts in 1977 to complement other Victorian Main Street buildings. The false front has a bracketed cornice and four-paned windows with colored transoms. Roberts encouraged in the 1970s the renovation of several Main Street façades, charging owners a nominal fee of $300. A preservation enthusiast, Roberts has pitched Park City to the National Endowment for the Arts based on the fact that it is "one of the few communities with intact nineteenth- and early twentieth-century buildings and a still vital economy."

Adjacent to the deli, now Main Street Photographer, is the McLaughlin Building.

41. McLaughlin Building (523 Main Street)

The widow of attorney Frank J. McLaughlin built this rental property on the site of a burnt-out Chinese laundry shortly after the 1898 fire. In the 1910s Joseph Kemp, an English-born miner, lived here with his wife Emily, followed by Sabatine and Martha De Angeles who ran a billiard parlor called the Star Club. D. L. MacDonald, M.D., rented the space in 1925. Dry cleaner Harold Graham later acquired the building "as a homestead" for back taxes. Remodeled in the 1970s, the two-story frame building features a central upstairs window topped by a decorative opening. Notice the indented entrance on the street level flanked by display windows. Photographer Nick Nass, who has been in Park City for over twenty years, has a studio upstairs and developing lab downstairs.

Continue south past a small walkway between the buildings to the Queen of Arts gallery in the old Smith Building.

42. George Smith Building (515 Main Street)

George Smith re-built his 1885 butcher shop one month after the 1898 fire for $1,000. His new building boasted a roomy, well-ventilated ice chest which he financed with a new cash-only policy. The following year he was elected mayor. In 1903 Smith installed one of the Park's first electric signs, and during the next twelve years he expanded the building to the south and took in Alonzo Brim as a partner. The butcher shop became "Smith and Brim" until Smith died in an auto accident in 1919. The building was then leased to George Hoover who painted a star over the Smith and Brim sign and operated the Star Meat and Grocery into the 1940s.

The next old building along this row of commercial structures now houses Pleasures and LeAnne's Gifts and Leathers.

43. Paull Brothers Grocery (511-513 Main Street)

Built in the 1910s, this building provided additional room for a booming grocery and hardware business two doors south. Thomas H. and Charley J. Paull were old-time Park residents who had worked for mercantilists Berryman and Rogers and traded on the side to save money to go into business for themselves. In 1917 hard times forced the brothers to retreat to their original south store front, leaving the building here vacant until George Hoover, owner of the Star Meat and Grocery next door, opened the Hoover Apartments in 1941.

Continue next door.

44. King Residence (509 Main Street)

This simple false-front frame structure, built around 1905 on the former site of Thomas Clawson's saloon, was the residence of electric light technician Day E. King and wife Mary until the light company sold the building to attorney Henry Fares in 1915. Summit County established its sheriff's offices here in 1931. The old jail bars are still stored inside. Later it was used as a museum and as Chamber of Commerce offices. Privately owned since 1983, it now houses Cabin Fever, specializing in cards and novelties.

Continue past the new two-story brick building to the empty lot where Peter "Mac" McPherson built his trendy second-hand store called The Racket in 1891. Mac filled his display window with mannequins, which at the time was revolutionary. Both the *Park Miner* and the *Park Record* were appalled, although the *Record* later criticized the *Miner* for continuing to give this "splendid business" a "black eye."

The Racket was rebuilt after the fire and thrived for seventeen years. Park City business tycoon Quom Nom Low de Grover operated the People's Pool Hall, Chicago Cafe, and Utah Cafe here until his death in 1926. His son Joe, who immigrated from China in 1918, opened Grover's Cafe in 1927 but abandoned it for Colorado thirty years later. The building was crushed by heavy snowfall in 1972.

The next building on the right, past Fifth Street, is a deep, multi-storied, wooden-slat structure.

45. Sutton & Company Store (461 Main Street)

Utah natives Edwin D. and William D. Sutton worked at the Ontario Mine until they opened a butcher shop here in 1890. During reconstruction after the 1898 fire the brothers ran a temporary meat market out of the Union Pacific depot. Their retail space, which was decorated with flowers and evergreens and included a large side porch where open-air Park City Military Band concerts were held, was augmented by warehouses for hay and grain and a sausage factory that took up an eighth of this block. William ran the business's daily affairs, especially after his brother who suffered from miner's consumption moved to Provo. Although they did over $100,000 in sales in 1900, when William moved to Salt Lake City in 1920, later to be elected state treasurer, his managers drove the company into receivership. Trustees closed the store in 1924.

The north portion of the building with the gable roof is original to 1898 and cost $3,000. The southern portion is a 1907 addition. Both share a cornice line, but the upper-story window openings are higher in the original section. Notice the diamond-shaped Masonic opening under the gable. The Suttons were leading Masons and provided meeting rooms in the upper story while the lodge was being completed. Because other social organizations met here as well, the building was known as Social Hall.

Depression-era Parkites also found aid at the Public Welfare Office located in the building's northern half. The building was later used for apartments and as a branch of Granite Furniture. It is now Park City Shirt Company and Park City Artworks.

Next door, with the large hanging marquee advertising "The Club," is the McEwan Building.

46. McEwan Club Building (449 Main Street)

Built around 1905 between Sutton's butcher shop and the Silver King Restaurant, Frank McEwan's Club was a popular watering hole. Notice the detail in the architecture, including dentiled molding, brackets below the cornice, and elaborate wood lintels.

McEwan's Club emerged on the former site of E. P. Clarke's business block, completed in 1887, which provided a space for Thomas Brownell's candy store and Charles A. Tewksbury's hardware, as well as Frank McLaughlin's law offices. In 1907 the building shared a wood porch with the two buildings to the north. In 1917 the Prohibition Act forced McEwan into the billiard parlor charade, and he finally sold to L. J. "Heinie" Hernan, who operated The Club from 1920 to 1970.

When Hernan took the reins, The Club was ostensibly a soft-drink parlor but was closed in 1921 for selling alcohol. When it re-opened, Hernan reportedly had kegs behind a second-story wall panel attached to weights and pulleys. Booze was also stored on the rafters of the building next door. In addition, buttons under the bar warned prostitutes of impending raids. Heinie otherwise did not allow women into the bar, insisting on strict moral principle. The Club eventually absorbed the other half of the building which once housed the Silver King restaurant and later the Vienna Cafe. After Hernan's February 1970 death Josef Buehler restored the pressed tin-and-copper ceiling by removing residue from coal heating. He also recreated Hernan's extravagant wildlife taxidermy. In the 1980s Cooper/Roberts Architects designed a matching second-story for the left single-story building and a unifying porch to combine what had once been two buildings.

A single company now runs The Club and The Alamo next door. Both were shut down by state liquor officials for two weeks in 1992. A bartender had poured directly from a bottle instead of using the regulated measuring device. The Club caters to a young resort crowd, with a downstairs bar open for lunch and an upstairs bar open from 6:00 p.m to 2:00 a.m. Downstairs patrons are seated at a rectangular marble counter surrounded by an ornate brass rail. Next door is The Alamo.

47. Utah Independent Telephone Company (447 Main Street)

The intricate brickwork of this Mission Style façade is among the most interesting in Park City. The building itself was built in 1906 for the Utah Independent Telephone Company which folded five years later. The company competed with Bell Telephone, each maintaining its own set of differently colored telephone poles. Utah Power and Light occupied the building from 1919-27. When it became the Windsor Billiard Hall in 1927, it narrowly missed being destroyed by the fire that

Utah Independent Telephone Company, detail (I. 47)

decimated the Blyth Fargo "Big Store" next door to the south. An unsteady business, Windsor Billiards opened and closed several times between 1927 and 1942.

Bob Dean, a Salt Lake City school teacher, bought this structure in 1968 and named it The Alamo because it resembled the famous Texas fort. The architecture is an amalgamation of Spanish Colonial Revival with Queen Anne brickwork. Notice the copper window frames. The interesting interior ceiling is a series of barrelled vaults. The Alamo, a locals' beer hall, has a pool table and other trappings of a neighborhood bar.

The next building to the south, with pastel lotus stalks over three sets of double doors, is a Works Project Administration building, now a hand-craft mall, restaurant, and bar.

48. War Veterans Memorial Building (427 Main Street)

During the Depression the federal government sponsored building construction to provide work for the unemployed, including this 1939 Art Deco building. The War Memorial honored Summit County veterans of the Spanish-American and First World wars and was used originally as a recreational center with a gymnasium and spa. In the 1970s federal assistance again provided for renovation, and city officials acquired it with intent to move their offices here.

Sam Ascheim's mercantile preceded the Memorial. The Wal-Mart of its day, it was filled from deck to ceiling with "everything a man, woman, or children [could] wear or consume." It was destroyed by an arsonist in 1881 and replaced by a sandstone building with an elaborate second-story Masonic lodge room. Aschiem's nephew Solon Spiro, of Spiro's Tunnel mining fame (located above the Park City Ski Resort), came from Manhattan, and together they ran the store as the "Count" (Sam) and the "No-Account" (Solon).

After the 1898 fire, when Spiro took a job representing Schlitz beer in the Philippines, Robert C. Chambers acquired principal interest in the mercantile which was then known as The Syndicate. In 1902 it became the Blyth Fargo "Big Store" with Sherman Fargo as manager. It burned down again in 1927.

When the city ultimately moved its offices to the Marsac elementary school above Main Street, it sold the Memorial building to Bob Savin who gave it a $2 million makeover. The city stipulated that the building could be used for retail, hotel, or office purposes but restricted restaurant and entertainment space to 15,000 square feet. The nightclub "Z" Place was founded by Steve and Debi Scoggan, Savin's daughter and son-in-law, who struggled with a fickle market until Savin managed to secure a suspension of restrictions in 1992, opening the entire building to club activities. But the dance floor was so large that it never seemed full, and the club gave way to "Z" Treasure Trove in 1994.

Continue south past the brick building at 425 Main Street to the ornate wooden portico with the Flat Rabbet Framing marquee.

49. Oliner Tailor Shop (421 Main Street)

Joe Oliner moved a 12-by-36-foot house from Empire Canyon to this location after the 1898 fire to use as a tailor shop. He added a window in front and made other alterations. In the spirit of well-intentioned multi-culturalism, the *Record* noted: "This is the Jewish holiday known as Roshashonah [sic] and Joe Oliner being the only Sheeney in town has closed his shop to celebrate the event." Peter Osika, a Polish immigrant who billed himself "the Leading Union Tailor" to curry trade union favor, bought the shop and operated it from 1908-12. Later German tailor August F. Marquardt worked here. It housed a barber shop in the 1940s. Note the curious decorative elements of the 1970s restored second level façade: the arched door, elaborate parapet, and window surrounds.

The adjacent brick building with the protruding display window and recessed entry was once the famous Oak saloon. The brick front is new.

50. The Oak (419 Main Street)

The pre-fire Gem Saloon at this location was operated by a man appropriately named Tom Collins. Morse Maranda re-opened the saloon after the fire and later sold it to C. Henry Spriggs and James Crooks, owners of a saloon in Eureka, Utah. They called it The Oak. Civic-minded Spriggs built a public bandstand for concerts next to the former Blyth Fargo "Big Store" site and rented his meeting space in 1909 to the Commercial Club, a committee that later reorganized as the city's first Chamber of Commerce in 1921.

Legend holds that Robert ("Butch Cassidy") Parker robbed revelers and gamblers at The Oak in 1910. Spriggs installed an armed guard afterward. If Parker and the Sundance Kid were killed in Bolivia in 1908, then someone else held up The Oak, though historians are undecided about whether Parker actually lived incognito in Washington state until 1937.

"Judge" Henry Shields ran his law office here in the 1910s. An Irish immigrant, Shields came to town to be the city marshall in 1879 after serving as a peace officer in Alta, Utah's, mining camp. A hard-nosed frontier marshal, Shields had previously faced charges of brutality. He served as Summit County judge during the 1880s and 1890s and facilitated the federal war on Mormon polygamy in the county. He died in 1919. This 1922 northern brick addition to the building is the only part which remains. The wooden frame section was destroyed by a 1974 fire. From 1976 to 1984 it housed *The Newspaper* which merged with the *Park Record* in 1983.

Next door is the Fire Memorial Park, which includes public restrooms.

Oliner Tailor Shop (I. 49)

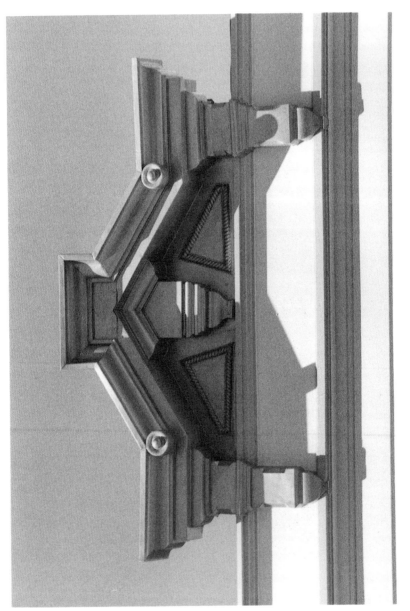

Oliner Tailor Shop, detail (I. 49)

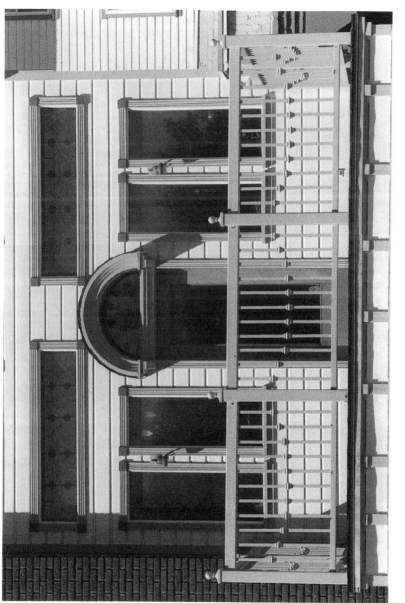

Oliner Tailor Shop, second story (I. 49)

51. Fire Memorial Park (405 Main Street)

In 1918 a fire started above Central Drugstore here. The building's tin roof created a furnace which impeded firemen who otherwise found their clothes freezing in January weather. An August 1973 fire destroyed four additional buildings here, including Poison Creek Drug, the *Park Record* office, and the badly-damaged First Security Bank (see next entry).

The park memorializes two other fire casualties, the Ontario Mill and the Silver King Coalition Mines Building. The Ontario was located across Main Street to the east, against Rossie Hill; the Silver King Coalition stood alongside the railroad tracks on lower Park Avenue and served as the terminal for the Silver King Tramway.

Continue south to the old State Bank of Park City, now Le Niche Gourmet and Gift Shop. Notice the arched windows and brickwork on the second level.

52. State Bank of Park City (401 Main Street)

This two-story building dates from at least 1916 and originally featured windows containing seventy panes of glass each. Henry Fares who owned several Park City rentals, owned the building. His wife had opened a millinery at this site in October 1898. In 1916 Fares sold the property to John C. Cutler, governor of Utah, who deeded the property for a "State Bank" branch office in Park City. The State Bank became First Security Bank in the 1940s. Though the building was damaged in a 1973 fire, the burglary-proof vault and 1870 safe survived. Three years earlier two Salt Lake City men broke into the bank through a brick wall from an adjacent realty office and, unable to crack the safe, got away with only $1,300 in loose change. They were arrested when a police officer recognized a letterman's jacket taken from the service station where they had stolen acetylene torches.

Next door, The Shirt Off My Back (405 Main Street), a wooden structure with a cone-shaped tower and ornamental balcony, was probably built by William J. Buch as a real estate investment about 1923. It later became Decker Jewelry Store. The façade has been newly renovated.

Continue south across Fourth Street to the building with the wooden balcony extended across the sidewalk, now Quicksilver clothing and skiboards.

53. Davis Building (363 Main Street)

William H. Bennett, Park City police officer, fenced this corner with quaking aspen poles for one of the city's earliest makeshift buildings in 1873. He replaced it with a newer two-story structure ten years later. Bennett rented to everyone from doctors to saloon keepers. At the time of the 1898 fire the Palace Restaurant was operating here.

After the fire Bennett sold the property to Fred R. Davis, the local school district treasurer. Davis built a 1,000 square-foot, two-story frame building with a shed-style roof and wood cornice. Around 1910 Charles W. Hodgson opened a store here that sold jewelry and expensive banjos, shaving mirrors, fountain pens, and china. When the Main Street Marketplace Mall was constructed behind and around this and adjacent buildings, the façades were preserved but the rest replaced.

The adjacent green building with white trim, now Rocky Mountain Christmas Gifts, was the Wells-Fargo Office.

54. Wells-Fargo Express Office (355 Main Street)

This string of three buildings (363, 355, and 347 Main Street)—typical of mining town structures—housed the Wells-Fargo Express offices in the center portion until the 1920s when it was taken over by the American Railway Express Company. The latter added a stone addition to the rear to house a vault. The two-story frame building has a wood cornice connecting it to the building to the north, once a residence used by merchants. The red frame building to the south was one of the *Record*'s many offices over the years. Only the front façades remain of these buildings which have otherwise been incorporated into the Main Street Marketplace Mall.

55. Main Street Marketplace Mall (333 Main Street)

This is the house that Debbi built. Renowned cookie queen "Mrs. Fields" and husband Randy met and married in California where Debbi became convinced of the positive value of cookies after prescribing them for depressed friends. With $50,000 from her husband, Debbi opened a cookie stand in Stanford. When customers didn't flock in, she took her product to the streets, luring in customers with a technique she called sampling.

Her faith in cookies, combined with a proselytizing zeal, turned her single store into an empire. The Fieldses were attracted to Utah's family values and work ethic and decided that Park City was the perfect setting for their family business. Debbi, an indefatigable supporter of charities, donated a percentage of her profits to the Cystic Fibrosis Foundation and brought the Utah Symphony to Deer Valley for summer concerts.

Randy Fields's investment company Silver Mill planned the Main Street Marketplace Mall (originally named Silver Mill Mall) to house the cookie headquarters, to serve as a testing ground for Debbi's retail experiments, and to provide space for a select group of retailers who would complement her vision. Randy's original plan was turned down by city officials who thought the design too "Disney-esque," "cutesy," and unlike anything else on Main Street. Park City's Historic District Commission at the time favored architecture that complemented but did not replicate neighboring designs. The debacle left Debbi disillusioned, victimized by oldtimer/newtimer sensibilities, and she threatened to take her business elsewhere. Fortunately the Fieldses and city officials met and were able to reestablish violated trust. The present construction features a variety of massing, form, height, and setback, all meant to offset the impact of height.

Meanwhile Debbi opened a cookie college to train managerial acolytes, started an experimental restaurant called "Spike's Grill" in the mall's upper floor, purchased La Petite Boulangeries from Pepsico, and opened a candy factory and ice cream parlor on Main Street in the old Dudler brewery where she also housed the cookie collegians. Her privately-owned company went international and boasted 600 outlets at its peak. Randy, with his vision of a year-round Park City economy, planned an industrial park geared toward high-tech businesses at the intersection of Interstate-80 and U.S. Highway 40.

Financial analysts point to the Fieldses' desire to maintain direct control over their outlets as one of the reasons their financial base crumbled in 1989. They also point to a failure to diversify, despite Debbi's dabbling in other retail forms. The company's first-half 1988 earnings fell by 96 percent. By 1993, when Fields had lost her European stores, Prudential Insurance Company moved in with a bailout, retaining Debbi as chair of the board which now makes all company decisions. As for the mall, it passed like the Egyptian Theater into Resolution Trust Corporation hands.

Historically the mall occupies space where the Woodside Store once stood, an older if no less paternalistic corporation which supplied miners with almost everything they needed. At first employees were issued coupons and later credit which was deducted from their paychecks. The Ancient Mariner Gallery is among the current tenants.

The next building south of the mall, a wooden structure now bolstered by cinderblock and brick, was site of Shields General Store.

56. Shields General Store (323 Main Street)

Irish immigrant Charles Shields was one of the Park's first prominent local businessmen. He opened a general store here in the 1870s where his line included groceries, stationery, and the "Chinese Must Go" brand of cigars guaranteed to be "white labor" produced. John joined his brother Charles in transforming the store into Shields Brothers in 1886. Both men also served terms as mayor. When the 1898 fire consumed the old store, they erected a new one within one month. They later rented space to Madame O'Hara and Garvin Millinery, one of the city's many female-operated businesses. The site was re-built about 1926 and the present structure completed in 1991. It currently accommodates Tiff's and C & C Indian Art galleries.

Next door at 317 Main Street, the Eating Establishment opened in 1972 on a lot formerly occupied by the Independent Club, Senate Cafe, and M. L. Condon's New Grand Hotel. Open for breakfast, lunch, and dinner, the Eating Establishment features regional themes: meat loaf, skillet dishes, and omelettes.

Next door, the two-story building with dark brick and an ornamental iron balcony, is the Bardsley Building.

57. Bardsley Building (309-311 Main Street)

This 1925 building was constructed for general medical practitioner William J. Bardsley on the former site of a drugstore. Bardsley lived with his family on the second level and served the community beginning in 1903 for almost fifty years. The building sat vacant in the 1950s, while in the 1960s a beauty parlor occupied the space. The entrance on your north leads upstairs to the Bearlace Cottage linen and antique shop, while Jim Stewart's "The Painted Pony" studio is on the street level. Stewart, an art teacher, bought the building in 1971.

At the Meyer and Lido galleries next door—the old Silver King building—notice the ornate fan lights, brick pilasters, and oval portholes. Inside the Meyer gallery is the original hand-painted, iron bank vault and an original brick wall. The Lido has an original copper ceiling.

58. Silver King Mining Company (305 Main Street)

The Crescent Mining Company Office stood on this spot until the 1898 fire. The Crescent Mine on Pinon Ridge, run by Edward Ferry and the Michigan Bunch, was once the richest in the district. A narrow-gauge railroad called the Crescent Tramway ran from the depot at the bottom of Main Street (the Silver King Coalition Building) to the mine. At first the cars were horse- and mule-powered and descended by means of two brakes in each car controlled by hands and feet attached to ropes. Accidents were frequent. The tramway paved the way for the town ski lift. Thomas Kearns of the Silver King Mining Company and later a U.S. senator purchased this lot in 1898, tore down the Crescent building ruins, and constructed one of the first post-fire brick structures here. It housed the Silver King offices and the First National Bank, chartered in 1891.

The 2,500-square-foot edifice, designed by architect Fred A. Hale, has hollow, red-pressed brick walls, a stone foundation, an extravagant cornice, and arched windows. Although only one-story, twenty-foot-high walls give the interior a spacious feeling. It is divided in half by a brick wall and a joint vault designed to be burglar- and fire-proof. The vault, which is still there, rests on a concrete and stone foundation, is built of iron and steel, and weighs over ten tons.

The entrance was originally a side corner, where one immediately faced a counter spanning the building's width. At the rear was cashier Sam Kenyon's apartment with bedroom, wardrobe, and bathroom. The interior was done in natural woods, hard-finished plaster walls, and

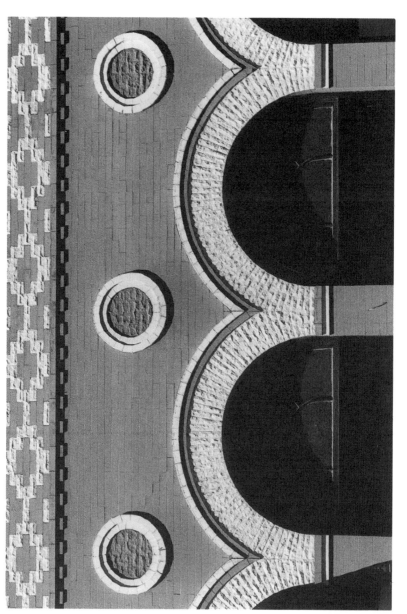

Silver King Mining Company, detail (I. 58)

Silver King Mining Company, vault (I. 58)

elegant "modern up-to-date conveniences." On the outside under the steps running up Fifth Street was a trap door to a stone coal cellar.

Only two months after construction cashier Kenyon was inspecting property at Utah Lake, fell into the water, and nearly drowned. Afterwards, in intense pain, he sent out for morphine, overdosed, and died. Prominent Utah entrepreneurs such as Orange J. Salisbury, John J. Daly, William J. McIntyre, and John H. Deming were pallbearers. The First National Bank survived the Great Panic of 1893, while Park City Bank went under.

Continue next door to the T.M.I. Shops and El Cheepo Southwestern Grill marquees.

59. Treasure Mountain Inn Condominiums (255 Main Street)

These condominiums stand on the former site of Welsh, Driscoll, and Buck's General Store—"Welsh's" for short—incorporated in 1898 with William J. Buck, a former North Sea whaler, as president. The two-story brick store was one of the largest at its time and the first furnished with electricity from "cellar to garret." The sign over the entrance read "Clothing, Furnishings, Boots & Shoes, Dry Goods & Notions." At the height of business Welsh's employed twenty-two men and women and traded $300,000 annually. It also featured the town's first gas pump. Buck died in 1926. His son Fraser resumed business until the store closed in 1954. The condominiums, constructed in 1964, represent the city's first effort at resort housing.

The Wasatch Brew Pub parking lot where you began is directly across the street to your left (east). This marks the end of the Main Street tour.

II.
Old Town Neighborhoods

DISTANCE: 2 MILES   TIME: 3 HOURS

This tour begins at the parking lot next to Wasatch Brew Pub (250 Main Street) and proceeds south up the hill along Main Street to the turnaround, then north down Park Avenue to Eighth Street. The return trip takes you south on Woodside Avenue to Fifth Street, east to Rossie Hill, then back to where you began. If, toward the end of the tour, you find the hillside stairs fatiguing, you can easily return to the parking lot at any point.

As you walk through these historic neighborhoods, your attention will be drawn alternately to either side of the narrow streets according to address. In old Park City street numbers sometimes lack synchronization for opposite sides of the streets. For instance, when you are at 151 Main Street you will be one-half block from 150 Main Street. At one time Park City's street designations were changed so that Third Avenue became Fifth, Second became Sixth, and so on. None of this should confuse you if you follow the suggested itinerary.

Treasure Hill to the west and Rossie Hill to the east of Main Street comprised Park City's first residential areas. Proximity to the business district implicated these neighborhoods in the 1898 fire, though a few structures survived on Park's and Woodside's western avenues and on Rossie Hill's Ontario and Marsac avenues to the east. When residents rebuilt, they constructed the crosswing plan cottages popular at the time as well as the more classically-lined four-square plan houses just coming into vogue. You will notice the general demographic rule that miners located close to the canyons, while merchants and professional people lived farther north, though there were many exceptions.

Historically upper Main Street consisted mostly of boarding houses. For decades miners were forced by law to live, unless married, in barracks operated by mine owners on company property. When the city council released them from this restriction in 1901, the result was a boarding house boom. The Bogan, Royal, and Alaskan are examples of such hostelries.

Boarding house residents were mostly eastern and southern European emigrants since northern Europeans, who had been in the city longer and assumed less physically demanding occupations, preferred Park Avenue which shared with its New York City namesake a reputation for affluence and style. Park Record *publisher Sam Raddon and merchant William Sutton were two local notables who chose the avenue's loftier heights. Also chapels were built*

OLD TOWN NEIGHBORHOODS

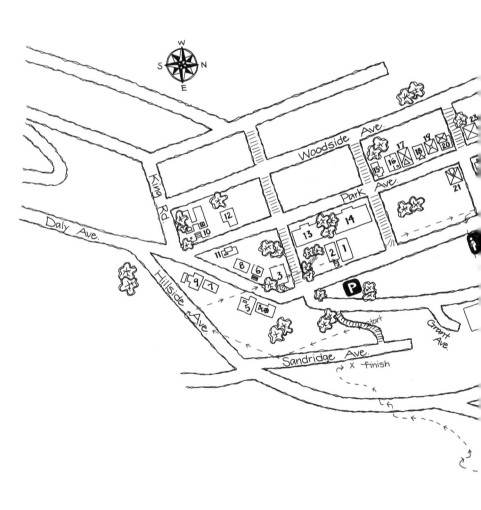

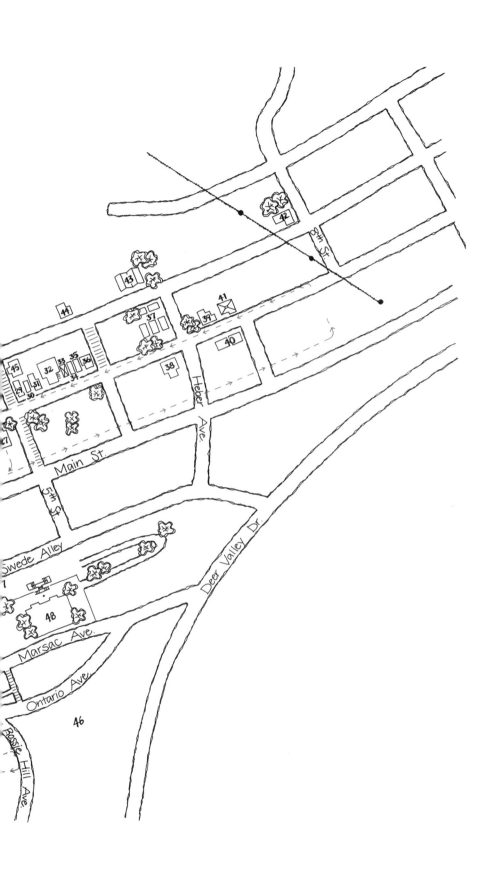

there away from canyon and mining mill neighborhoods where drunkards, prostitutes, and bootleggers reigned.

Just south of the Wasatch Brew Pub on the west side of the street is the first stop on the tour: the cream-stuccoed Mediterranean-style Star Hotel which was once the Grover residence. On the street level is the Moriarty Hat and Sweater custom design shop.

1. Grover House (227 Main Street)

Originally this building was the home of Joe Grover, son of Quon Nom Low de Grover. Born in San Francisco in 1857 and relocated to Park City in 1889, Quon Nom Low weathered intense discrimination, prompting him to change his surname. Yet he built one of the largest real estate portfolios of any Parkite. He made three trips to China during his life where he met his wife and fathered Joe. His wife never came to the United States. At de Grover's death, the *Park Record* eulogized him as a community pillar who took special interest in children's education and recreation. Joe emigrated from China in 1918. During the 1930s he renovated the home's façade and opened a hotel, though the present style reflects a 1970s facelift.

Next door to the south, the four-story Imperial Hotel, with the Park City Coffee Roaster at ground level, was originally the Bogan Boarding House.

2. Bogan Boarding House (221 Main Street)

John Bogan moved to Utah from Illinois in 1887 and built here around 1904. This is one of four intact historic boarding houses on upper Main Street. Like early student dormitories, boarding houses were supervised to keep miners' free-wheeling lifestyles in check, though after being granted their freedom they generally chose to continue living here for convenience and economics. Housekeeping for single miners was considered among the lowest Park City occupations.

Bogan owned the Bogan Mine, which the Silver King Consolidated Mine Company later acquired, and Geneva Stewart ran the boarding house. She advertised furnished, steam-heated rooms by the day, week, or month. In 1918 the house served as an emergency hospital during the flu epidemic. The building remained with sons John and James until 1925. In 1940 a fire burned the roof, and in 1974 the building was officially condemned though not razed. It was later restored and used once again for long-term lodging as the Imperial Hotel. Notice the stone foundation, the Dutch-curve gabled roof, the full-length upper balcony, and the decorative posts.

Continue up Main Street past the small park and children's playground to your right, noticing on your far left the view across Swede Alley of the nearly-collapsed house and barn just south of the saltbox-

Bogan Boarding House (Il. 2)

roofed house at 147 Swede Avenue (ca. 1880s). The four-story brick building to your right on Main Street with the two-story glass porch, now Grappa Italian Restaurant, was the Royal Boarding House.

3. Royal Boarding House (151 Main Street)

Jennie Peterson ran this turn-of-the-century tenement house. Built before 1898, it is noteworthy for having survived the fire. In the 1920s it passed into the hands of Joe de Grover and then in 1928 to Justo Uriando, an Italian emigrant. When Uriando purchased another boarding house up the road, the Alaskan, in 1923, he was unable to retire a construction and repair lien against the Royal and it was repossessed in 1940 by the American Building and Loan Company. The rock wall is original, the concrete porch a later addition.

The current occupant, Grappa Restaurant & Cafe, open for dinner, features northern Italian cuisine. Diners top off their meals with an imported wine liqueur for which the restaurant is named.

On the southeast corner of Main Street and Swede Alley, the small 1880s shack at 186 Main Street was once a candy store. Farther to your left where the street bends is an ornate 2.5-story white clapboard house with blue trim.

4. Durkin Boarding House (176 Main Street)

Like Bogan, Joseph Durkin constructed a miners' hostel after the boarding house law was revoked. When he first arrived in Park City in 1876, he worked at the Ontario Mine, a company which employed him for twenty-seven years. Durkin also served on the city council. After marrying and moving to Prospect Avenue, he showed empathy for his bachelor colleagues and entered into the housing trade, dying in 1903 of lung problems. The house is a rectangular building which at one time included a large kitchen and ten sleeping rooms. Windows and doors were placed asymmetrically, and the house had wooden cut-outs and decorative jigsawed corner and trim pieces which were often manufactured and sold mass-market, both features of Victorian influence.

The Durkins kept the house until 1911 when they sold it to the de Grovers for Joe's headquarters. The interior was rebuilt during a 1970s remodeling. Notice the cupola and ornate woodwork in the brackets and cornice peak.

Next door, the yellow clapboard house with the metal roof is the Louder House.

5. Louder House (170 Main Street)

Missouri-born blacksmith James M. "Curly" Louder built this 1.5-story frame rectangular house as a blacksmith shop and residence soon after his arrival in Park City in 1882. According to Raddon's *Record*,

Durkin Boarding House (Il. 4)

Durkin Boarding House, detail (II. 4)

Durkin Boarding House, detail (II. 4)

60

Curly was a good smithy. He and his young bride Emily lived and worked here until 1889.

Kate Carpenter and husband Frank bought the house in 1896 and turned it into a boarding house. Mary Cunningham, who owned a house farther up the hill at 139 Main Street, purchased and later sold the Louder House to Dominic and Mary Giacoma, owners of the Giacoma Building and Dudler Brewery on Main Street. The Giacomas owned the red-shingle rectangular house two doors south at 158 Main Street and the Rowe House next to it at 150 Main which they used as rental properties. Notice the old central chimney in front of the gable. The large perpendicular extension to the stem-wing is an unusual but not un-heard-of historic expansion.

Continue south. On your right, the dilapidated rectangular house behind the deteriorating rock wall is the Cunningham House.

6. Cunningham House (139 Main Street)

Thomas and Mary Cunningham built this one-story frame hall and parlor house around 1885. Thomas moved to Park City in 1878 just six years after the camp's founding, worked at the Ontario Mill, later in the Daly and King mines, and died in 1905 from the pandemic black-lung disease that afflicted miners. The Cunninghams owned other rectangular houses as well, which they rented to mining families.

Proceed to the Rowe House on the left, unmistakable for its second-story overhang across a broad front porch.

7. Rowe House (150 Main Street)

An English silver miner born in 1850, Nicholas Rowe lived here with wife Carrie, sixteen years his junior, and two sons. Rowe came to the United States in 1869 followed by Carrie twenty years later and built a one-story house here in 1885. They later took the ambitious and unusual step of adding another story. Perhaps they contemplated entering the boarding house business.

The broad 2.5-story Alaskan House across the street to your right still has a hanging marquee.

8. The Alaskan Boarding House (125 Main Street)

This red, frame 2.5-story rectangular house was another home for miners who wanted to live close to town. John and Sarah Anderson who operated the Alaskan during the 1910s and 1920s were Swedish and only rented to northern Europeans. Many of their tenants filled low-end service and white-collar jobs as lunchroom managers and railroad clerks. When the Andersons let the property go in 1928, it passed into the hands of Italian Justo Uriando, the unfortunate owner of this and the Royal who lost both to the bank.

Up the street on your left, recently renovated with the white fence, is one of few remaining historic two-story crosswing cottages in Park City.

9. Sullivan Cottage (146 Main Street)

James and Mary Sullivan bought this property from Thomas Cunningham in 1892 and took out a $500 construction loan the same day. It was owned by Sullivan descendants into the 1960s. They also owned rental houses next door which are no longer there. Notice the eclectic Victorian trim over the lower-façade front window.

Continue south to the five-point intersection of Main Street, Park Avenue, King Road, Hillside Avenue, and Daly Avenue. There is a good view of Main Street and Silver Creek one block up Hillside Avenue to your left, should you want to take a short detour. Otherwise make a sharp right, crossing the street onto Park Avenue to double back in a northerly direction. The grade is a little steep initially but evens out quickly.

Immediately to your left, St. Mary's marks our first stop. The imposing church, built of unpolished limestone, sits high above a tall rock wall. After St. Mary's we will encounter other historic churches and homes, as well as modern condominiums, on both sides of this narrow avenue.

10. St. Mary's of the Assumption Church (115 Park Avenue)

Irish Catholics comprised a substantial part of Park City's early boomtown population. At first a traveling priest celebrated Mass in Simon's Hall where the Claimjumper restaurant now stands on Main Street. Then in 1881 Parkites began constructing their own church, the oldest Roman Catholic sanctuary in Utah. Grading for the lot commmenced in July and within a month the outer building was nearly completed. St. Mary's has two matching wings, a northern chapel and a southern classroom hall which the Sisters of the Holy Cross School first occupied. This was a branch of the order's midwestern school in St. Mary's, Indiana.

On 27 May 1882 Archbishop Ahmany dedicated the church and reportedly delivered such a convincing sermon that "the most pronounced atheist would give ear to his argument." The sisters opened the school that September.

The building was partially burned on 4 July 1884. Parishioners quickly restored the structure, finishing their efforts with a new bell installed in May 1885. The date on the church, 1884, refers to the post-fire renovation. Sisters added a music room for voice, guitar, piano, and mandolin lessons and opened a business academy the same year with courses in typewriting and shorthand, painting and drawing, and morality and discipline. The academy was principally for girls, while

St. Mary's of the Assumption Church (II. 10)

separate classrooms and playgrounds were maintained for the lesser Boys School. During the 1898 conflagration firefighters created a break with explosives to save the church. Then parishioners renovated for an Easter 1899 High Mass.

As Park City declined with the Depression, the school was forced to close in 1930. An additional crush came in the form of a fire on Christmas 1949. But parishioners refurbished again, installing a stained glass window above the high altar on the west wall. The window depicts Mary's Assumption and memorializes the community's faithful dead. A new organ was purchased with trading stamps.

The parish's dedication was partially recognized in 1970 when St. Mary's was added to the Utah State Register of Historic Places. The rock wall in front of the church is the oldest intact part of the structure and was considered a historic landmark as early as the 1940s. The building is still used as a sanctuary.

Across the street to your right, the little green frame rectangular house with pink trim situated nine steps down from street level was built around 1900.

11. Peterson House (104 Park Avenue)

Swedish emigrants Axel H. and Jennie Marie Peterson were two of this rectangular house's early occupants. Axel was a miner. Their neighbors originally included Charles Moore, a mining engineer, and wife Margaret; Joseph Artimo and Daniel Carma, Spanish miners who immigrated in 1916; Bert and Franco Franza, Italian brothers and miners; and Irish emigrant Emma McBride who ran a boarding house that catered to southern Europeans.

The Buck House, a two-story yellow frame home with brown trim, is on your left.

12. Buck House (145 Park Avenue)

William J. Buck immigrated from Canada in 1899 and managed the Main Street department store where Treasure Mountain Inn now stands. He and his wife Annie lived here in this two-story hall/parlor construction. Alfred Dadge, the department store's clerk, and wife Mary were neighbors.

Continue north, noticing the crosswing cottage on your left at 157 Park Avenue, a gray frame house with a metal roof. On your right, before the wooden stairs to Main Street, an early three-room school once stood. As you pass the stairs, notice the original rock foundation now supporting the Jefferson House Apartments.

13. Jefferson House Apartments (206 Park Avenue)

The second of three Park City primary schools named after U.S.

presidents, the Jefferson Public School was torn down in 1902 to make way for a larger brick school of the same name. Demolished again in 1935, re-built, and torn down in 1961 to make way for the Snow Palace commercial building, the apartments were built in the mid-1960s. They comprise part of the Treasure Mountain Inn Condominium complex next door to the north, the site of two historic residences probably built after the 1898 fire.

14. Treasure Mountain Inn (220 Park Avenue)

The Ed Prudence family lived next door to the Jefferson School. Prudence, an Ontario mine engineer, was laid off during the 1908 slow down and became a janitor at the Judge Building in downtown Salt Lake City, built by Park City mining magnate John Judge's widow. Prudence was killed that same year while inspecting an elevator shaft when the car unexpectedly descended and crushed him. The Prudence home later housed Helen Lanford's Cafe and Boarding House which was destroyed by fire in 1949.

Next to the Prudence family were George and Emma Moulding, English emigrants who met and married in Illinois and settled in Park City in 1879. George worked at the Ontario mine for twenty-five years, while his son, William E., was a Park City police officer in the 1910s-20s.

As you continue north, notice, past the sprawling Mine Camp Inn (245 Park Avenue), the historic 1880s rectangular houses to your left, for example the white house with blue trim at 259 Park Avenue. The distinctive placement, with the narrow side to the street, is a "shotgun plan." This particular house has a central chimney. Past the wooden stairway on your left is the Lawrence Boarding House.

15. Lawrence Boarding House (305 Park Avenue)

This 1900s high-Victorian-style home, one of Park City's few, was John and Mary Lawrence's boarding house through the 1920s. The Lawrences were Irish and kept mostly native-born American miners. In 1984 Barbara and Ken Martz restored the house. The upper story, destroyed by fire and repaired with an ill-fitting roof, was restored by the Martzes to its original appearance.

Continue down the hill past the new condominiums on your right to two significant historical buildings on your left.

16. St. John's Lutheran Church (323 Park Avenue)

A private residence since 1973, this simple but dignified church was erected in 1907 by Pastor O. H. Elmquist who was himself a master carpenter. The Lutheran community consisted of nine Swedes and twenty-two Finns, so services were held in foreign languages until 1920 when English was introduced. Because the congregation lacked a resi-

Lawrence Boarding House (II. 15)

dent minister, members met only once a month. Regular services stopped in the 1940s, and the church was abandoned. Renovations in the 1970s and 1980s changed the sanctuary and backroom into bedrooms.

Next door, the 2.5-story Victorian domicile with the porch-pediment flagpole was the residence of Park City newspaper magnate Sam Raddon.

17. Raddon Mansion (325 Park Avenue)

Samuel L. Raddon worked for the *Salt Lake Tribune* before moving to Park City in 1884. By summer the next year his name stood alone on the *Park Record* masthead as editor and publisher. He brought with him his infant son, Sam Jr., whose mother died twelve days after childbirth. In 1888 Raddon married his sister-in-law Louisa Harper and reared six other children.

Ten years later the great fire destroyed Raddon's original home and his recently-completed Main Street printing press, and he and his family moved into Herbert W. Deighton's house while they rebuilt. Deighton, owner of the Palace Meat Market on Main Street, was related to Raddon's first wife Clara. In 1906 Raddon was dealt a blow when his second wife Louisa died.

As a teenager, Sam Jr. worked for his father setting type, running presses, and writing news stories. In 1911 he and his wife Elizabeth honeymooned in Portland, Oregon. They liked it so much they stayed, Sam in the employment of the *Oregonian*.

Sam Sr.'s daughter Mary lived in this house for a time, but the home was later abandoned until John and Nicki Price, southern Californians, renovated it beginning in 1970. They also renovated St. John's Lutheran Church. Notice the interesting wall and roof-line angles and the stained glass windows. Two upper-level doors open onto a full-length balcony.

The vacant lot north of Raddon's house was site of the Methodist Episcopal Church. George Jayne founded the congregation in 1885 by holding revival meetings in Ontario Canyon. He netted a one-day conversion record of twenty-nine souls. "If Mr. Jayne could have more assistance," observed Raddon's *Record*, "we are of the opinion that a great moral reformation would sweep this town." They built here the same year. As with nearly everyone else after the Great Fire, the Methodists were forced to rebuild in 1898.

Proceed to the house just north of the vacant lot.

18. Holt House (339 Park Avenue)

Theodore P. Holt replaced a burned-out cottage with this two-story four-square plan in 1900. Notice the square shape of the house and the pinnacled, four-sided roof—known as a pyramid—which are typical of

Raddon Mansion (II. 17)

Raddon Mansion, detail (II. 17)

many of Park City's four-square houses. Fred W. Post, a mining pumpman, lived here with his wife Retta in the 1920s.

Next door is a 1.5-story four-square house.

19. Wilcocks House (343 Park Avenue)

After the 1898 fire, this house was moved from Deer Valley by Walter Wilcocks, an early real estate entrepreneur. Chaplin and Marianne Cone bought and restored it in the early 1980s. Notice how the roof resembles a French mansard design.

One door farther down the hill on the left is the Kescel House.

20. Kescel House (351 Park Avenue)

City merchant James T. Kescel rebuilt this stately eight-room, four-square house within a month after the great fire. It was later rented from Kescel by miner Joseph L. Christensen and wife Rita.

Continue north past the rear side of Main Street Marketplace Mall (on your right) to the corner of Fourth Street. The newly-renovated red frame house with the ornate porch to your right was built in 1902.

21. Bennett House (364 Park Avenue)

A four-square plan home, this renovated structure was built by William H. Bennett, city police marshall, after his original house was destroyed. It varies slightly from standard four-square forms in its rectangular shape and asymmetrically-arranged façade. The porch retains some of the original lathe-turned porch piers and decorative brackets. Compare it to the equally ornate but more standard four-square massing across the street at 363 Park Avenue.

Bennett was an activist who used his police powers to realize his vision of the city, which included harassing Chinese launderers to abandon Main Street. After the fire Bennett left town for ranching. Sam Raddon lamented during the clean-up, "How long do you suppose Bill Bennett would have allowed those decaying carcasses of horseflesh to remain a stench in the nostrils of pedestrians on Main Street if he was still Marshall of this town?"

In 1899 Bennett exchanged the open range for the convenience range and began selling "Home Comfort" stoves, later selling his house to Charles Heath, a bank clerk.

Across Fourth Street to the north on Park Avenue, the brick chapel on the right with a prominent corner tower and fishscale cone is the old Congregationalist Church.

22. Congregationalist Church (402 Park Avenue)

Congregationalism was Park City's first active Protestant sect, with

Kescel House (II. 20)

Congregationalist Church (II. 22)

a chapel here already in 1879. In the basement the New West School provided fifty students with a liberal arts education in such subjects as Latin and philosophy. Tuition was $1 per month. After the fire a tent was erected until the new church could be rebuilt in 1899. The old brick walls, which had survived but were unstable, were ordered razed.

With the mining slowdown, Congregationalist and Methodist congregations merged in 1919. Since then the church has been served by Methodist ministers as the Park City Community Church. The building was restored in the 1970s with many original furnishings intact—the pews and altar, for example—including an old-fashioned pump organ. Soon after restoration, a dog, accidentally locked inside after services, destroyed some interior decor. Several days later the city held a charity slave auction and the minister's wife "bought" the mayor and commanded him to prohibit dogs from worshipping unattended. In 1995 the city prevented the congregation from stringing a banner advertising Easter services until a public outcry prompted a reversal.

Among the many interesting aspects of the eclectic architecture, notice the variety in window shapes—gothic, rectangular, and triangular. Artist Pete Park created a stained glass window for the church in the 1980s, a "Tiffany-styled autumn pastoral scene." Its text from Psalms 121:1 read: "I shall lift up mine eyes to the hills, from whence cometh my help."

Across the street to your left is the Diem House.

23. Diem House (401 Park Avenue)

John Diem, Main Street's saddler, constructed this balloon-frame house in 1899, a larger, more rectangular version of the square-massed, pyramid-roofed home. Balloon frames were popular with wealthier merchants and usually boasted a greater range of external decoration.

Continue north. The one-story "pyramid" at 405 Park Avenue was built in the 1890s and housed Edna Hershiser, a miner's widow. On your right at 416 Park Avenue is another home originally occupied by a single woman.

24. Shield House (416 Park Avenue)

Margaret (Mary) B. Shield constructed and owned this large four-square house. A Miners' Hospital nurse, Shield kept a lodger, Chauncey Smith, who was a mining motorman, to help make ends meet. Shield was a leading advocate for miners' health issues throughout her life.

To your left, the 2.5-story home at 421 Park Avenue, with dormers at right angles, was constructed in 1898. It is a larger variant of the four-square, similar in depth to Diem's house. Notice the fishscaled pediment in the wrap-around-porch roof. The stone root cellar and northwest corner are later additions.

To your right is the original Park City Mormon chapel, now the Blue Church Lodge.

25. The Blue Church (424 Park Avenue)

From the start Park City Mormons were viewed as only slightly more human than Chinese and were officially locked out of mining employment. A vigilante "Loyalty Legion" trashed 1880s Mormon leader Gad Davis's modest home behind Dodge's Saloon on Main Street. Mormons were considered disloyal to the United States, and the federal government confiscated their property, drove their leaders into hiding, and forced the church to the edge of bankruptcy over issues of polygamy, secessionist tendencies, and rejection of federal officials.

Mining companies lifted the embargo on Mormons in 1894. At that time Margaret Mason donated these two lots for a meeting house which was completed in 1897. It was destroyed by fire the next year, rebuilt in 1899, and opened for services in March 1900. An addition to the rear was made between 1926-30, and in 1938 work began on an adjoining Amusement Hall. Unlike many of the post-fire buildings prudently built with brick, Mormons constructed a wood-frame Gothic-inspired chapel, the largest historic post-fire frame building still partially visible.

The church passed into private hands in the early 1960s. It was renovated in 1977 as a ski lodge with care taken to preserve the door, window openings, and pews, and was subsequently one of the first Park City buildings placed on the National Register of Historic Places.

A tragic 1982 fire destroyed all but portions of the façade. The latest restoration, completed in 1984, replicated the original gothic architecture and building materials as well as the distinctive blue tones. There is an interesting Victorian influence in the oval dormer window which is surrounded by fishscales. The weathervane and stained-glass panel above the front door were preserved. A Jaccuzzi took the place of the baptismal font.

To your left, the blue wood and cinderblock structure is the King Duplex.

26. King Duplex (437 Park Avenue)

This building was occupied in the 1920s by Day King, power and light company manager, and wife Mary, who had previously lived in the Main Street sheriff's office. Frank M. and Jeanie Stone lived in the other half of the duplex. Stone was a mines mechanic. Notice the bungalow look, though it has a pyramid roof and an unusual cut-away balcony on the second level.

Continue north past the Blue Church Townhouses on your left and neighborhood parking on your right to the Pink Cottage on the east (right) side of the street.

27. The Pink Cottage (450 Park Avenue)

This simple dwelling was rebuilt on the site of a rectangular house burned out in the 1927 Blyth Fargo fire. It had housed John Simonetta and John Foderaro, Italian immigrant miners.

To your left, 445 Park Avenue is a relatively ancient rectangular house built in 1882. Continue north to the two-story, recently renovated crosswing cottage on your left.

28. Pike House (463 Park Avenue)

Arland Pike, mining engineer, lived here with his wife Bertha in the 1920s. As you walk by, notice the saltbox slope to the roof on the back side. The house was recently given a new foundation.

Just past the wooden steps on your right is the LeCompte House on your left.

29. LeCompte House (501 Park Avenue)

Edward P. LeCompte was one of Park City's earliest doctors, famous for inscribing patient records on his Main Street office wallpaper. Every year when his office was re-papered his books were cleared. LeCompte spent much of his free time at the Deer Valley racetrack, after serving in George Armstrong Custer's Seventh Cavalry. He built on this lot in 1888 and was forced to rebuild ten years later after the fire. One of the avenue's finest homes, it boasts that deeper, rectangular shape which provided more room for wealthy folk. Notice how the rear gable slopes off like a saltbox roof. LeCompte shared the house with wife Lydia into the 1920s.

To your right, 502 Park Avenue is another four-square residence built around 1905 with a truncated roof.

Two doors north of LeCompte's house is the Bardsley Cottage.

30. Bardsley Cottage (517 Park Avenue)

Another doctor, William Bardsley practiced on Main Street for half a century beginning in 1903. He lived with his wife Martha in this rambling two-story cottage, with the gable end facing the street shotgun plan.

Episcopal Reverend Stephen C. Clark lived between the two doctors in a house that was identical to LeCompte's, though no longer standing. The Reverend had easy access to the chapel which sided the Bardsley Cottage to the north.

31. St. Luke's Episcopalian Church (525 Park Avenue)

"The problem in Park City is distinctly social," wrote a visiting Episcopalian church official in 1929. "The wretched Church on the hill is never going to make an impression on that Godless town. Services can be carried on for the faithful. But the Church should have an attractive hall, accessible to the boys and girls of the city, where decent substitutes can be found for the immoralities that are flaunted in the faces of every one."

The town's first church was constructed in 1890 up the hill at 310 Park Avenue, with assistance from prominent local Episcopalians Horace C. Bates (a druggist) and Samuel L. Raddon. The one-story, frame, Gothic structure before you, the "wretched church on the hill," was built in 1901 on the former site of Dryman Hall, one of the town's earliest public schools destroyed in the fire.

The Episcopal church's fortunes declined steadily at the turn of the century as membership fell from fifty-nine in 1897 to seventeen in 1907. The Park mission was abandoned, the church deconsecrated in 1947, then revived for a short while in 1960. Attempts to restore the chapel began in 1978, after which it was reconsecrated for services to the present.

The blue cottage next door at 527 Park Avenue belonged to a single mother, Julia F. Byrne, an Irish emigrant. Her son James F., born in the states, supported the family as a grocery salesman. The four-square house at 539 Park, built in 1903, reveals another variant form of construction with its truncated gable eclipsing the pyramid shape behind, rather like one large dormer.

Farther north, the massive hammered-limestone building with a steep-pitched, dormered and belfried-roof is the old Washington School.

32. Washington School (543 Park Avenue)

First named Central School, this impressive frontier edifice was constructed in 1889 of limestone quarried in Peoa approximately ten miles northeast. It was one of few buildings to escape the 1898 fire. Built on four levels, it originally contained three large classrooms and an expansive foyer which rose up three stories to the belfry. The first of three local schools built in the 1880s and 1890s, this is the only one still standing. It was renovated in 1903 to accommodate more students but closed in 1931 during the Depression due to declining enrollments. It was sold in 1936 to the Veterans of Foreign Wars (VFW) for $200 and used as a social hall until the 1950s when it was vacated.

The VFW sold the building in 1970 to Environetics Corporation which donated the exterior to the Utah State Historical Society for restoration. Environetics maintained ownership of the interior and in 1984 opened a twelve-room hostel, the Washington School Inn. It has been honored as one of 200 select Great Inns of America and given a four-diamond rating by the Automobile Association of America.

The building's stunning carved-wood bell tower is capped by an attractive witch-hat dome and flagpole. Notice the wooden window sills and hip knobs on the dormer pediments.

Washington School (II. 32)

Washington School, detail (II. 32)

Next door, the cement and wooden two-car garage was site of Julius and Eva Frankel's house. Julius, born in Germany and brought to the United States by his uncle, Sam Ascheim, in 1885, worked for his uncle's store and at the Ontario mine and then opened his own clothing store in 1896 on Main Street.

Their next door neighbors were the Andruses.

33. Andrus House (553 Park Avenue)

Stonemason Gideon Andrus and wife Jane lived here ten years beginning in 1900. A Main Street tailor, William Osika bought the house in 1913 and stayed almost twenty years. Notice the coal-chute door in the cement foundation.

The vacant stretch across the street to your right once belonged to Charles Barnicott who rebuilt in October 1898 following the fire. Barnicott was born in England in 1830, immigrated to the United States at age thirty, and arrived in Park City in 1879. The house stayed in the family into the 1930s. A couple of lots north of the Barnicotts, the old Park Hotel once extended from Main Street to touch Park Avenue.

To your left, the blue metal-hipped structure is the next stop.

34. Hurlburt House (557 Park Avenue)

This substantial, cropped pyramid-roofed house with the unconventional off-center entrance was home to prominent druggist Edwin Damon Hurlburt and wife Connie. Born in Cheyenne, Wyoming, in 1878, Edwin's father opened a store in Park City in 1900. During Prohibition Ed was fined for selling alcohol and moved to Santa Barbara to open a hotel. The house was renovated in 1986 by Bonnie Deffenbach who renovated other Park Avenue residences at the same time.

Notice the nine-paned window transoms to the left of the door and the porch-cornice lathe work typical for the period. Next door, the green house with red and tan trim is the Fennel Cottage.

35. Fennel Cottage (561 Park Avenue)

This was John and Maggie Fennel's 1.5-story residence. John was a pre-Prohibition liquor merchant, which guaranteed a respectable income. Notice the diminutive window at the attic level. The bay is probably not original.

During the 1900s the Stringer family, Thomas and Mathilda, lived next door at 569 Park Avenue with six children in a squatty rectangular house. Thomas was a mine assayer. Scottish miner Robert M. and Ellen Miller lived in the L-shaped crosswing cottage at 575 Park Avenue.

Next door to the Millers is the Westfield home, partly concealed by the pink garage addition.

36. Westfield House (581 Park Avenue)

William P. and Mary W. Westfield resided in this circa 1890 eclectic house. Pennsylvania-born William came west with Ascheim's nephew Solon Spiro to manage Ascheim's shoe department. When store owner-ship changed, William continued working at the Blyth Fargo store until fire destroyed it in 1927, then participated in a short-lived partnership in Zack Oblad's Quality Shop. He died in Park City in 1940 at age seventy-nine. Notice the unusual side entrance portico, the probable result of a later remodeling.

Continue north past the vacant lot on your left once owned by prominent merchant Thomas J. Cupit and wife Rebecca who emigrated from England in 1875. Thomas owned a Main Street cigar and sundries store and was a major Odd Fellows benefactor. The Cupits moved to southern California in 1920.

To your right, past the alley leading to Centennial Park, is a string of houses built around 1905. They share a variant four-square plan with truncated gable roofs. Originally single-walled, they have since been improved with studding.

To your left is the new Motherlode complex.

37. Motherlode Condominiums (621 Park Avenue)

One of the significant homes that once stood along this section of the block belonged to Barney and Fannie Riley. Barney was born in Ireland in 1847 and worked as a miner in Park City beginning in 1876. When he broke his leg at the Ontario Mine, he decided to go into the saloon business with George Morrison and later Patrick H. Towey. When Towey died of miner's consumption in 1908, Riley retired, but remained a presence in town until his death in 1917.

To your right, on the corner of Heber Avenue, is the Concrete House, now yellow with blue trim and occupied by Café Mercato Mediterraneo di Nonna Maria.

38. Concrete House (628 Park Avenue)

Named for its solid cement construction, the Concrete House pre-dates the 1898 disaster and halted the fire's spread down lower Park Avenue. Willis Adams, the photographer who captured underground mines, lived here. He died in 1930. Willis Ritter, Adams's nephew and Utah District Court chief judge, used this house as a second residence and left it to his son William who worked at the mining mills. Ritter was a controversial judge whose stay of serial murderer Gary Gilmore's execution was overturned by a midnight appeal to Denver's Circuit Court.

In the 1940s the house was occupied by less respectable tenants. Maureen "Ma" Foster ran a hotel here which was busted in 1956 as one of the last Park City houses of ill repute. In the early 1960s George

Despain catered to a new form of recreation with his Timberhaus Sporting Goods. Despain was among the first full-line skiing outfitters when Park City turned born-again boom town. The current occupant, Café Mercato, specializes in gourmet foods and features live music. The eastern wing is a more recent addition.

To your left, the dirt-lane extension of Heber Avenue is where the 1883 Crescent Tramway, a narrow-gauge railroad, carried ore from Pinon Ridge beyond Treasure Hill to the depot at the base of Main Street. Just north of the lane, on your left, is a small park where the likes of William C. Berry, a bartender; Lewis Girard, millman concentrator (separated silver from other minerals); and James C. Wiley, a liquor merchant, lived. George Huddy of Main Street's Huddy Brothers operated a neighborhood grocery here.

Farther north on your left is the Nelson house.

39. Nelson Cottage (651 Park Avenue)

This cottage was built around 1925 for Lila Nelson, daughter of Colonel John A. and Eliza Nelson, two of Park City's prominent turn-of-the-century entrepreneurs. Their estate comprised Nelson Hill near present-day Park City Ski Resort where they donated land for Miners Hospital and for Glenwood Cemetery easement. Born in Virginia City, Nevada, where her parents had mining interests, Lila opted for a more civilized east-coast habitat where she was treasurer for a theater chain. But she later settled in Park City, dying here in 1939. The house remained in Nelson family hands until 1953.

Across the street to your right, now the Broken Thumb Grill (690) and Go Big clothing (698), are two former Kimball Duplexes.

40. Kimball Duplexes (690 and 698 Park Avenue)

A string of similarly-designed single-story hall/parlor houses was built here around 1885 by Edwin Kimball as rental properties. During Park City's economic boom periods, when an influx of laborers demanded immediate housing, rentals could be profitable. Notice that each building has two doors placed symmetrically between windows, suggesting that each structure consisted of two rectangular houses attached on one side.

A non-Mormon, Kimball operated a mining supply company, served a term as mayor, and surprised residents in 1886 by offering his name as selectman on the Mormon ticket. Non-Mormons did not generally associate with the People's Party, the Mormon church's political arm, and Sam Raddon actively supported Kimball's Liberal Party opponent. After his defeat Kimball moved to Salt Lake City and died of "apoplexy" (a stroke) in his childhood home in Massachusetts while vacationing there in 1893. His widow Geneva managed his real estate holdings until 1917.

To your left, the 2.5-story light-green house with a gabled-bay addition was built by Ellsworth Beggs.

41. Beggs House (703 Park Avenue)

This home was constructed in 1906, although the concrete foundation was added later—the house lifted and the foundation poured underneath. Ellsworth J. Beggs, a carpenter, married Eva Jane Lockhart, daughter of prominent capitalist Oliver C. Lockhart. Ellsworth later acquired an ore mill and served as a city councilor. Meanwhile Eva led the Women's Athenaeum charitable and cultural society. The Beggses resided here until 1946 when they sold the house to a banker.

Next door, the Kimball-owned livery was originally part of the Beggs lot. It was converted into George Stonebreaker's National Auto Garage from 1915 until 1942 when Stonebreaker moved to Evanston, Wyoming. The National Garage name is still faintly visible across the wooden façade.

At this point you may return directly to the parking area if you would like by retracing your steps south on Park Avenue one block, turning left at Heber Avenue to Main Street, and climbing five blocks south. Continuing the tour will take you on a scenic but more circuitous route, with three more points along the way where you may opt to return directly to the parking lot should you find the hills too challenging.

Proceed north under the ski chair lift and mining company tramtower ruins to Eighth Street.

The city has lately considered turning Eighth Street into a Town Lift ski run. Turn left on Eighth Street and walk west one block uphill to Woodside Avenue. Houses began appearing on Woodside around 1881 when water mains were extended up Treasure Hill. Only two blocks from Main Street, Woodside Avenue was nevertheless considered a suburb. In fact, the 1899 *Record* warned women and children about venturing this far because of roaming farm animals.

On the southwest corner of Eighth Street and Woodside Avenue is the L-shaped McDonald residence, now slightly weathered but once considered a grand edifice.

42. McDonald Mansion (733 Woodside Avenue)

This spacious home was identified by Utah architectural historian Phillip Notorianni as one of three historic Park City "mansions" still extant, along with Raddon's and Sutton's homes on Park Avenue. Built around 1904 by Thomas J. McDonald, the house has a sophistication unique among the Park's straightforward, practical homes, yet is simple compared to the grandeur of Salt Lake City's period mansions. A carpenter, McDonald probably constructed the house himself. He came to work in the mines in 1874 and married Margaret Mawhinney,

McDonald Mansion (II. 42)

daughter of mining engineer Robert Mawhinney. The couple later moved from Park City when Thomas took a job with the Utah State Road Commission to oversee the earliest highways.

Turn left and proceed south on Woodside Avenue under the ski lift. The house to your left, fifteen steps down from street level at 664 Woodside Avenue, is a turn-of-the-century construction that housed a mining father and son.

Continue south. The grade will be a bit steep for another block and a half.

If tired, you can follow the path to your left (just past 658 Woodside) that becomes Heber Avenue and intersects Park Avenue and Main Street, either of which will take you back to the parking lot where you began.

Up the hill to your right, 633 Woodside Avenue was the home of George E. Hedges, a mining bookkeeper and public school teacher. James and Rhoda Berry lived next door at 627 Woodside with their six children. James managed the Kimball Livery and Stages on Main Street. Both the Hedge and Berry houses were 1885 crosswing cottages. Two houses up, on your right, is an earlier 1880 rectangular house at 605 Woodside. Next door to that is the Old Miners' Lodge.

43. Old Miners' Lodge (615 Woodside Avenue)

Michigan Bunch entrepreneur Edward Ferry built this lodge as a single-miners' boarding house in 1889. Originally a narrow, two-story structure with dorm style rooms and—to the rear—a kitchen shanty, an outhouse, and a blacksmith's barn, a second addition was built on the north side after the 1898 fire. The construction employed a wooden balloon frame with square nails and dimensional lumber salvaged from surrounding mines. Electricity and indoor plumbing were installed in 1912 and 1919, respectively.

In the 1920s the lodge catered to married miners and was converted into small apartments. In the 1960s it operated as Park City's first licensed "motel" when a third addition was added to the back. In 1983 Hugh Daniel and Jeff Sadowsky bought the lodge and restored it as a bed and breakfast inn. It currently features ten guest rooms.

Continue up the hill. On your right is the Maloney dwelling.

44. Maloney Cottage (543 Woodside Avenue)

Malachi and Lizzie Maloney, Irish mining immigrants, came to the United States in 1884. Their sons represented the success of many second-generation Americans, Lawrence becoming a telephone electrician and his brother Thomas a pharmacist. The house was probably moved to this spot, since it first appears on maps in the 1890s when rectangular houses were rarely built. The T-wing was probably added around the time the house was moved.

Old Miners' Lodge (II. 43)

Proceed south nearly to the top of the hill. To your left is a good view of the bell tower topping the Washington School Inn. A bit farther south, to your right, is the 1890 crosswing cottage of Daniel H. Haran and wife Katherine at 501 Woodside Avenue. Haran managed several Main Street saloons during the city's early years.

Continue south past Interline Condominiums on your left at 524 Woodside Avenue and, to your right, the large wooden quonset structure with newer condominiums at 475 Woodside above the street level.

Looking again to your left, you will see the Hamilton home with rustic blue and brown trim.

45. Hamilton Cottage (502 Woodside Avenue)

A crosswing cottage-by-addition, this structure was originally a simple rectangular house built in 1885 by Russell C. and Elizabeth Hamilton. After migrating from England, Russell worked as a miner and the Hamiltons crowded eight children and several boarders into this small space. They found it necessary to add a crosswing around 1900.

Next to the Hamilton house is a flight of wooden stairs on your left leading to Park Avenue. (If you encounter the condominium complex at 470 Woodside Avenue, you have gone too far.) From the top of the stairs you can see the old Marsac School across the Main Street gully, about even with your elevation. Built in 1936, this Depression-era Public Works Project reflects the Art Deco style of the period. Notice the use of brick and terra-cotta, the hard-edged and angular massing, the flat roof, and the decorative cornice.

Carefully descend the stairs and turn right onto Park Avenue. Proceed south one block to Fourth Street, turn left, and head east between the church and Bennett house to Main Street. You'll see the China Steps ascending Rossie Hill across the gully directly in front of you.

46. Rossie Hill

The knoll east of Main Street was named after the town of Rossie, Michigan, home of the Michigan Bunch which included Edward Ferry, David McLaughlin, and other early Park City capitalists. At the crest, Rossie Hill Drive was once an extension of Heber Avenue. Ontario, Marsac, and Sandridge avenues follow lower slopes. At first the hill had a tonier reputation than Park Avenue, but after the 1898 fire more laborers' homes were built on the east side and Rossie took a back seat to Park Avenue. In the 1970s Rossie again became a sought-after residential site and several characteristic resort-style A-frame chalets now dot the hillside.

If you are not feeling up to Rossie Hill, you can follow Main Street south to the parking lot. Otherwise continue as follows.

Cross Main Street (you will pass the Barking Frog on your right) and continue east down Fourth Street to Swede Alley (formerly Farrell Alley). Cross Swede Alley and continue toward the stairs. The multi-level China Steps Municipal Parking Structure, constructed with $1.3 million in Park City Redevelopment Agency and Marketplace Mall financing in 1986, is to your right. The parking lot/alley to your left just before the China Steps is a vestige of Grant Street and the area once known as Chinatown.

47. Chinatown (Grant Street)

Originally a dirt roadway, Grant Street was once a bustling ethnic neighborhood. Asians came to the western United States in the 1860s to work on railroad lines, and many formed communities in boom-towns such as Salt Lake City where Chinatown was located just south of the present ZCMI Center on Plum Alley. A Chinese community developed in Park City around 1880 and became the object of intense alienation by those who considered the Chinese heathens.

As early as 1881 Parkites inaugurated a campaign to drive oriental businesses and residences off Main Street and over Silver Creek to Grant Street. The *Park Record* revealed a glimpse of humanity when editorializing against malicious boys who threw stones at the hapless Chinese. But such empathy was mitigated by a bridge constructed by the Marsac Company from Main Street—across Grant—to Rossie Hill, "obviating the necessity of going through Chinatown which has been very disagreeable for the ladies." You can see the bridge's one-time destination near the top of the cement retaining wall on Rossie Hill. The bridge was not a grand structure but more of an "inclined wooden footpath," according to early Sanborn insurance maps. During the bridge-construction period, Edward Ferry evicted a Chinese commercial tenant whose business had burned down and was rebuilding. A quasi-official policy relegated the Chinese to a contained ghetto.

In 1882 the newspaper urged citizens to avoid gambling and opium dens across the creek and suggested that Chinese govern themselves. When the Chinese hoisted a flag, other Parkites were "indignant at having such an emblem flapping in the pure atmosphere of Park City."

In 1886 citizens held a meeting in the Congregational Church to argue the question, "Must the Chinese Go?" The debate pitted two seemingly racist public school teachers against two more liberal attorneys. The lawyers carried the debate by quoting freely from the "Preamble to the Constitution" (actually the Declaration of Independence) and the country's "Magna Carta" (written five centuries before the United States was conceived).

Despite the lawyers' performance, the Chinese question did not go away. The next year city officials strengthened China Bridge and the *Record* called for an ordinance to legally limit heathen businesses to the other side of the creek. A fire in a downtown laundry confirmed Sam Raddon's belief that Chinese businesses were "dirty, unhealthy fire traps and a blight on Main Street." Mayor and cigar-maker Charles Street christened one of his signature brands "'Chinese Must Go' Cigars." Officials brought many Chinese to trial for running opium parlors, though no law then prohibited it.

In 1892 the *Record* announced that it was pleased to see that "negroes" were taking over the predominate Chinese occupation of porting, adding: "The *Record* hopes to see the day when not one of the [Chinese] race can make a living in the camp and it commends the reform now inaugurated." Meanwhile police marshall William Bennett raided wash houses and imprisoned Chinese who lacked business licenses.

The Great Fire of 1898 did not discriminate, and in some ways it became a watershed for better ethnic relations. Chinese accepted assistance from the ecumenical Women's Relief Committee, and the twentieth century marked the rise of several prominent Chinese merchants and businessmen such as real estate mogul Joe Grover and Senate Restaurant owner Charlie Chong. All that remained of Chinatown after the fire was China Bridge, which stood until 1954 when it was reduced to China Steps.

Park City histories have romanticized the Chinese ghetto and other ethnic neighborhoods. The Finns, Cornish, Welsh, Slavs, Swedes, and Irish kept their own streets, their own saloons and boarding houses, and all disliked trespassers. There was little cohesion until after the fire when Mormons and gentiles, Brits and Slavs, wealthy and poor began to see themselves as a common community. The fact that Parkites clung together to "help their own" illustrated changing times. Today, far from racial prejudice, the town's divisions are along "local" and "part-timer" sensitivities.

Climb the China Steps. At the parking lot and parking structure driveway, pause momentarily to notice City Hall, occupying the old Marsac School, to your left (north). Notice the building's raised torchlike emblems topping each pilaster and portico corner, creating a crenelated, or castle-like, effect.

48. Marsac School (431 Marsac Avenue)

The firm of Carl W. Scott and George W. Welch, noted for designing most of Utah's public school buildings during the Depression Era, designed this mid-1930s New Deal edifice. Scott apprenticed under architect Richard Kletting, known for the Utah State Capitol and Park City's Utah Power and Light building, among others. Scott himself designed the Masonic temple and South High School in Salt Lake City.

The Marsac School was constructed on land formerly occupied by the Marsac Mining Company's mill.

The New Deal subsidies of U.S. president Franklin D. Roosevelt were popular in Park City. As a one-industry mining town, the community was especially hard-hit by the economic downswing. Public Works construction sites provided jobs for out-of-work miners. To provide materials for Marsac Elementary, the Jefferson and Lincoln schools were demolished and cannibalized. Marsac contained an unprecedented twenty-four classrooms, with faculty offices, an auditorium with a cyclorama stage for scenery changes and velour curtains, and an integrated automatic clock and bell system. The *Record* reported that City Hall staff members decorated an unusual Christmas "tree" here in 1986: a mature marijuana plant. They later harvested and then smoked it in the nearby restroom. Suspects claimed they thought it was a tomato plant and were keeping cuttings for starts.

Continue east across Marsac Avenue to the continuation of China Steps. Marsac was an unimproved dirt roadway without an outlet until well into the twentieth century. Access by foot paths or stairs was once typical for higher residential areas. At the base of China Steps is a house to your left at 402 Marsac Avenue, an example of truncated-roof, four-square styling. Built in 1902 of single-wall construction, it was later improved with a studded-frame.

Ascend China Steps to the intersection with the red sandstone walkway midway up the hill. This pedestrian sidewalk follows a path marked on maps since the first residential construction on Rossie Hill but never designated as an avenue.

Turn right and proceed south along the walkway to the end. The houses facing this sidewalk have Ontario Avenue addresses, which is the next street east. The earliest homes were mostly crosswing cottages, representative of 1880s construction, such as the cottage toward the end of the walkway at 341 Ontario.

Returning to China Steps, notice the green, yellow, and rust-red four-square house to your right at 355 Ontario Avenue, built without stud-framing and later reinforced. Notice the variant design which includes a recessed porch and other asymmetrically-arranged façade features.

You may descend China Steps back to Swede Alley and continue south to the parking lot if you would like. Otherwise continue with the tour.

Turn right and continue climbing China Steps to the top. The view here is as good as it gets unless you are on a ski slope. At the top, where the "Stairway" sign is posted, turn right and follow Ontario Avenue south. You'll notice, on your right, several steep footpaths leading to homes on the sandstone walkway, followed by newer homes blending with their historic neighbors below.

Continue on Ontario Avenue, keeping to your right as it merges

402 Marsac Avenue

402 Marsac Avenue, detail

Sandstone walkway, Ontario Avenue

with Rossie Hill Avenue. Follow the long, steep, downward curve to the intersection with Marsac Avenue.

At Marsac Avenue, cautiously turn right and head north to the wooden steps that ascend the hill. Instead of climbing these steps, carefully cross Marsac Avenue west to the unpaved neighborhood parking area.

Cross the parking area to the telephone pole with the "Public Parking" sign attached to it. Although this narrow alley is unmarked, you are on a section of Sandridge Avenue whose historic homes lining the hill's edge are all 1880s rectangular houses, many of which have been expanded into crosswing cottages. To your right, the green-, orange-, and rust-colored cottage at 228 Sandridge was occupied by Nichols Tanauer, a 1902 German immigrant, and family.

Across the asphalt sidewalk (a section of Sandridge Avenue), next to the streetlamp pole, are wooden and metal-grate stairs leading to Swede Alley. Descend the stairs, noticing the house to your right at 222 Sandridge Avenue. This was the home of Vitas and Elsa Sandstrom, Finnish miner immigrants. To your left, another cottage at 218 Sandridge was inhabited by a Swedish immigrant family who ran a laundry out of their home. Only about 10 percent of Park City's historic homes are on Rossie Hill since re-building after the fire took place mostly on the opposite side of Main Street.

At the base of the stairs, turn right. Ahead of you, directly east of the Wasatch Brew Pub, you can see the remaining southern section of Grant Street, once the hub of the Chinese ghetto. To your left is the parking lot where you began. This ends the Old Town Neighborhoods tour.

III.
Lower Town and Park City Ski Resort

DISTANCE: 2 MILES   TIME: 2.5 HOURS

This tour begins at the historic Miners Hospital, follows Park Avenue south to Eighth Street, winds back down Woodside, Norfolk, and Empire avenues to the Park City Ski Resort and Glenwood Cemetery, then back by way of Silver King Drive to Park Avenue. Parking is available at Miners Hospital which functions today as a community center.

The old hospital is located on the east side of Park Avenue, across the street from a fire station, set back some distance from the street behind a grassy promenade with flower beds and a fountain. At the street a wooden "City Park" marquee indicates the location, as does a Sullivan Road street sign. Sullivan Road, an alley, parallels Park Avenue and intersects the hospital driveway. On either side of the old infirmary, beyond parking areas, are recreation facilities: two picnic pagodas and restrooms to the south and an activities center and sports turf to the north. The hospital itself is an impressive example of Park City architecture.

1. Miners Hospital (1354 Park Avenue)

Modern hospitals look nothing like this three-story Victorian mansion. Warm red brick, full-height bays, and stone lintels give it a "bed-and-breakfast" appearance. The building's hipped roof camouflages its true height, while a box-style central dormer is flanked by double-dormered gables, balanced in the rear by a brick chimney reaching the same height.

This is not the hospital's original location. In November 1979 it was moved here in one piece from a knoll near the ski resort where the Shadow Ridge Condominium Hotel now stands. Eliza Nelson donated an acre of ground for the hospital in 1904, and construction and maintenance were financed by the sale of state trust property. Harry Campbell, a local contractor, served as architect. When the hospital was incorporated, the Western Federation of Miners (WFM) labor union purchased much of the stock.

The health risks associated with mining cannot be overstated. Those who survived cave-ins and explosions often succumbed to black lung disease, a variety of tuberculosis known as miner's consumption, or "miner's con," caused by inhaling metallic dust. The hospital was an important community institution. In mining states slave owners advisedly kept their human "capital" away from mineral excavations—one

Miners Hospital (III. 1)

Miners Hospital, detail (III. 1)

LOWER TOWN AND PARK CITY SKI RESORT

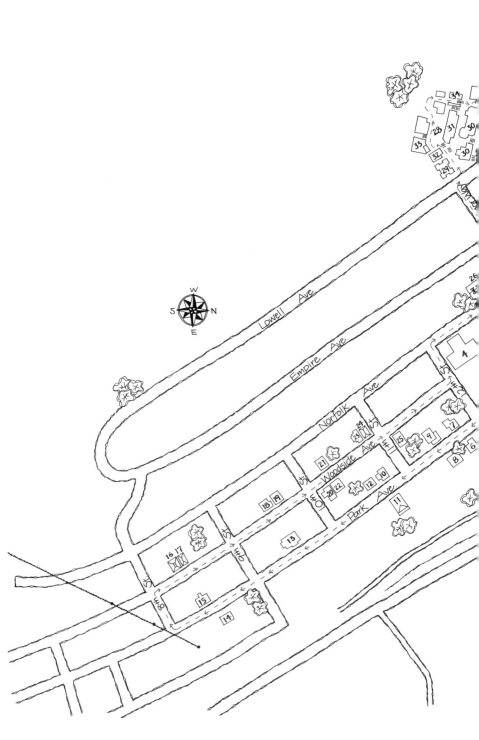

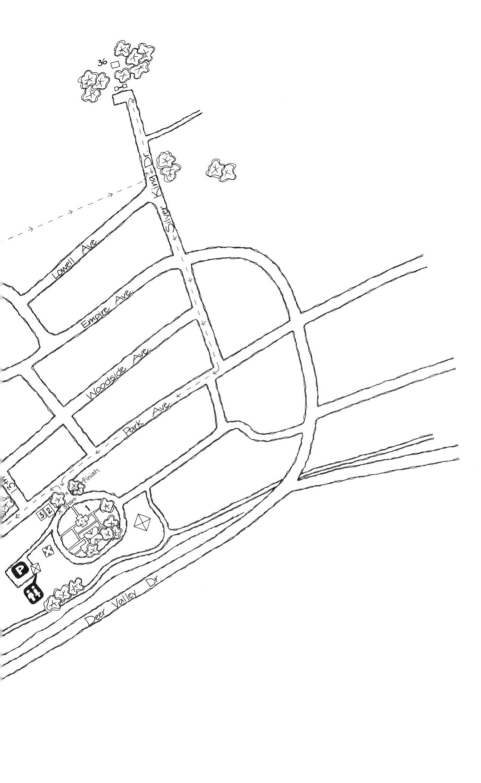

reason slavery never took hold in a major way in the intermountain west. Although a minority of early Utahns owned black or Native American slaves, they generally put them to work as domestics.

When the Spanish Influenza epidemic swept the United States in 1918, the hospital served to isolate flu cases, with the Rio Grande Depot used as an overflow quarantine area. City officials imposed a containment ordinance which prohibited anyone from appearing in public without a cotton-gauze mask. Saloon keeper Jack Murphy defied the ordinance, was arrested, sued for $10,000 for false imprisonment, and fell down a mine chute and died before the case was resolved. Nevertheless in one week alone in January 1919 ten Parkites died of influenza.

In the summer of 1919 the WFM engaged in an unsuccessful seven-week strike during which hospital donations, which were deducted at a rate of one dollar per month from miners' paychecks, were halted, throwing the hospital into a fiscal crisis. After the strike donations were voluntary. Workers rebounding from uncompensated unemployment found it impossible to shore up the institution's teetering financial framework. Meanwhile unpaid doctors and nurses threatened to desert, while mine owners blamed the union and the union blamed the mines. The hospital finally closed.

As a stop-gap measure, mine owners opened an emergency hospital in the New Park Hotel with free, limited medical services for emergency cases. This was a boon to accident victims but not to those who had advanced bronchial ailments. Sisters of the Holy Cross, who had staffed the hospital since 1904, stepped forward and purchased the building for $3,000 and kept it open until 1957.

When the University of Utah Medical Center was constructed in the 1960s, it was granted the Miners Hospital trust by the Utah legislature. Private physicians occupied the building itself and ran a clinic until the tourist boom in the 1970s when it was converted into an American Youth Hostel, later the Palace Flop House with rooms for $5 a night. In November 1979 preservationists encouraged its relocation, while developers planned its demolition. After wrangling over tax credits, owners eventually donated the building to the city, although the city could not initially agree on whether to wave total-height zoning requirements downtown. Finally the city council decided to move the building here, and the 400-ton structure was hoisted onto timbers, cables wrapped around it, and towed down the hill by a huge semi-tractor on a treacherous four-day journey.

In 1981-82 Salt Lake City architect Wallace Cooper was chosen to renovate the building for use as a city library. A proposed $750,000 bond received grass-roots opposition, which was not entirely surprising in a community whose library circulation ranked third lowest in the state. But Parkites later rallied in support and formed a "Book Brigade" to move the library collection hand-to-hand from its former Main Street location, 3,800 feet from here. The books were later moved in 1993 farther up the street to the old high school.

Today the building is used for public and private meetings, receptions, and recitals. During the day it is open to the public. The interior was redone in the 1980s to replicate the former fir trim with oak. An unfortunate yellow-slickered miner is said to still reside here, haunting the upper floors, a grim specter from the distant past.

After enjoying Miners Hospital architecture and grounds, walk west of the building to Park Avenue. Carefully cross Park Avenue to the west and turn left and proceed south. Notice the second house across the street to your left, a square-frame bungalow.

2. Maxwell House (1326 Park Avenue)

Elmer H. Maxwell was a rancher hailing from Oakley, Utah. He arrived in Park City in 1925 and built this bungalow which in plan conforms to the type but is missing the typical prominent porch. In Park City Elmer established the Maxwell Apartments on Main Street and sold Singer sewing machines. He originally squatted on land owned by the Ontario Mining Company and was unable to obtain a deed here until 1935. The bungalow style came into vogue in the 1910s-20s. Since this corresponded to a gradual downturn in Park City's mining and housing fortunes, only about eighteen Park City bungalows can be identified from this period.

On the same side of the road, two houses south on the corner of Thirteenth Street, is a blue hall/parlor plan home with a northern addition.

3. Condon Cottage (1304 Park Avenue)

David and Elizabeth Condon constructed a substantial rectangular house here in November 1881 soon after arriving to teach at the New West School. Notice the symmetrical openings on the main wing which identify the house as a crosswing cottage by addition. The Condons later built the New Grand Hotel on Main Street where the Eating Establishment now sits. After David died just before the 1898 fire, his widow sold the house to teamster William Cunningham whose family had been burned out of their old home. The Cunninghams added the wing around 1910. Main Street blacksmith Edward Berry bought the house in 1916 and his family occupied it into the 1970s.

Cross the T-intersection at Thirteenth Street and continue south on Park Avenue, passing the Coalition Lodge across to your left. You will pass a circa 1900 house on your left at 1274 Park Avenue, an example of later four-squares with an additional half-story and broad gable on the roof-face façade.

Farther up Park Avenue to your right, behind the brick and cement "Park City Library and Education Center" marquee, across a large parking area, is the seven-decades-old Art-Deco-style public high school-turned-library. It was built on part of the old city baseball park.

4. Winters High School (1255 Park Avenue)

Parkites bonded construction of their first secondary school in 1927 and named it, in Park City tradition, after U.S. president Abraham Lincoln. They later renamed it in honor of 1930s-40s school superintendent Carl Winters. When a new high school was completed on Kearns Boulevard in the mid-1980s, the city initially wanted to transform this building into a recreational facility but, in 1990, granted provisional permission to New York-based Northwest Investment Company to renovate it into an arts and education center with a new hotel next door. Residents objected. The city eventually funded renovation itself without a hotel. The structure now houses a modern library and extension offices of the University of Utah and Utah Valley State College.

Notice the terra-cotta ornamentation which enlivens the otherwise plain brick and cement. The matching building to the south was for school utilities.

Directly east of the library is a yellow house with brown trim.

5. Hansen House (1215 Park Avenue)

When Norwegian Arthur E. Hansen, a butcher, erected this large house in 1904, he over-extended himself and was forced to sell to Ephraim Sutton the following year. Sutton was owner, with his brother William, of a Main Street mercantile. He probably rented this property because he had moved for health reasons to Provo after the 1898 fire.

Architects classify this as a variant four-square plan covered by a clipped-gable roof. The lathe-turned porch tiers and brackets are original.

Continue south, crossing Twelfth Street, to see the wood bungalow with white trim across the street to your left, three houses from the corner.

6. Farthelos House (1150 Park Avenue)

A partner in Tony Polychronis's meat and grocery story on Main Street, Peter Farthelos built this one-story frame bungalow in 1921. It was originally located on Woodside Avenue and moved here in 1947 by a later owner, Clifford Street, son of mayor and cigar-maker Charles Street. The southside gabled vestibule is a later addition. The narrow lap siding, also called novelty siding, was unusual in Park City. The horizontal window bands and broad porch characterize bungalow design.

Directly across the street from the Farthelos house, on your right at 1149 Park Avenue, is a 1905 saltbox-roofed, rectangular house. This was a late appearance for this vernacular plan. Next door to the south at 1141 Park Avenue is an oversized 1890s variant of the popular four-square, and next door to that is the yellow, white-trimmed Clark House, a more typically square version of the same vernacular plan.

Winters High School (III. 4)

Winters High School , detail (III. 4)

Winters High School, detail (III. 4)

1149 Park Avenue

7. Clark House (1135 Park Avenue)

Peter Clark, a Scotch immigrant, had a long career as a bureaucrat. He originally worked as a miner but taught himself law and served as both county and city attorney and as the local Internal Revenue Service official. This 1895 house has a truncated hip roof and broad porch. The lathe-turned porch piers and balustrades are replicas.

Next door at 1129 Park Avenue, set back from the street on a narrow lot, is an 1890s rectangular house. Directly across the street is the Rolfe Cottage.

8. Rolfe Cottage (1128 Park Avenue)

The original portion of this 1895 house was constructed in shotgun plan—the narrow side facing the street. Charles Rolfe, a dairy farmer, added a wing in 1909, in this case as a stem wing because it was added to the original shotgun-aligned crosswing. Frank Archer, Main Street liquor merchant, and wife Theresa lived here from 1915-24.

To your right at 1125 Park Avenue is a true asymmetrical crosswing cottage from the same period. Past the picket fence to the south is the blue Walker House where skis form an X on the façade.

9. Walker House (1119 Park Avenue)

After David McLaughlin, principal property owner in the Park City Townsite Corporation, died in 1904, many of the corporation's properties were sold at auction. The Walker family, Ed and son Samuel, placed the highest bid for this lot where their original one-storied frame hall/parlor house was already standing. The Walkers were job printers. They added a second story in 1905 on first-floor walls that are noticeably deeper than the second floor's. The porch and garage are later additions. Another prominent family who resided here were Axel and Blanche Fletcher. Axel was a house painter and his wife Blanche was the unofficial town historian for decades.

Continue south on Park Avenue past the Valline framing gallery and cross Eleventh Street. The Brand-X Cattle Company Restaurant is across the street to your left. To your right, three houses from the corner, is the two-story wood-frame Houston House.

10. Houston House (1049 Park Avenue)

Nathaniel Houston was a life-long bachelor who made his living by building and renting homes for the city's transient community. He built this rectangular house in 1895 and sold it the next year to a miner, Albert Holindrake. Originally a one-story hall/parlor residence, John Brierly, who bought the house in 1906, added the second story with an evenly matched façade and rear roof extension resembling a saltbox. Brierly

Rolfe Cottage (III. 8)

Rolfe Cottage, detail (III. 8)

worked for Park City Consolidated Mining Company which had properties in Empire Canyon.

Directly across the street, in light blue with dark blue trim, is the Park's only example of a historic Craftsman bungalow.

11. Willis House (1062 Park Avenue)

This 1922 bungalow, with a broad porch under a low-pitched gable roof, reflects Craftsman style, which has recently enjoyed a renaissance. The simplicity was born of a late-nineteenth-century reaction against machine-generated uniformity, heralding a return to utility and an emphasis on materials. Craftsman features like the half-walls surrounding the porch reflect the desire for durable construction. Nothing is known of original builder Joseph Willis apart from the house itself.

Continue south on Park Avenue, passing an 1880s rectangular shotgun house that was later converted into a crosswing cottage (1043 Park Avenue, next door to the Houston House). Past the Alpine Shadows condominiums is an unaltered shotgun rectangular house at 1025.

12. Hansen House (1025 Park Avenue)

Like the Rolfe cottage, this two-story frame house is oriented shotgun-plan with the gable end set toward the street. Frank Hansen, employed by the Ontario Silver Mining Company, built here in 1893. Hansen emigrated from Denmark in 1868 as a Mormon convert and helped lead the precarious Park City Mormon community during its early years. He later returned to his native land as a missionary but, unlike fellow Mormons, engaged in mining upon his return. He raised a fortune in Alta, Utah, which he later lost through other mining investments. He also worked on the railroad. In 1902 the Hansens sold the house to William Armstrong, cashier for the First National Bank on Main Street.

The house next door at 1021 Park dates from the 1880s and is an example of the earliest, most uncomplicated four-square plans.

Continue south and cross Tenth Street. Across the street to your left is the Park Station Condominium Hotel. To your right, on the corner of Tenth Street, is a rectangular house dating from 1886 at 959 Park Avenue, followed by an original 1890 crosswing cottage at 949 and an 1880s rectangular house-turned-cottage at 943. These were all part of the Kimball family's vast real estate holdings.

The house next door at 937 with the saltbox roof was where town doctor and surgeon Thomas C. Clark lived in the 1920s. It was built by Charles Whitehead.

13. Whitehead House (937 Park Avenue)

This is a typically rectangular, symmetrical house, but the delicately

Hansen House (III. 12)

Whitehead House (III. 13)

jigsawed porch piers distinguish it. Whitehead, the original owner, worked in mining camps in South America, Australia, and throughout the western United States before becoming one of Park City's first settlers. He bought this land from the pioneering Snyder family and constructed the house in 1886. He worked for the Ontario Silver Mining Company as a drayer (freightman) and later as an accountant until dying in 1899 of an overdose of morphine which he took for rheumatism. Notable businessmen Sam Ascheim and Robert Chambers later held title to the house as a rental property.

A series of 1880s rectangular houses-turned-cottages is located farther south on your right at 929, 915, and 909 Park Avenue. Across the street to your left, the empty northeast corner lot at Ninth Street is where the Park City Heat and Light Company's power plant was located until 1910 when it was destroyed by fire. Electrical service was then taken over by Utah Power and Light.

Cross Ninth Street—a dirt driveway on the west side—to continue south past the Park Wood Condominiums on your right. Across the street to your left, the rectangular house with yellow corrugated metal-siding and red trim, now Zion's First National Bank, was once part of the Rio Grande Railroad's terminal complex.

14. Rio Grande Terminal (820 Park Avenue)

For years the Union Pacific Railroad Company held Summit County mining traffic in monopoly. John W. Young, son of Brigham Young, dreamed of constructing a railroad up Parley's Canyon to compete with the Union Pacific's line which ran from Ogden to Coalville within twenty miles of Park City. To raise capital, Young convinced a Spanish aristocrat to invest a million dollars in the railroad, luring him with maps of a non-existent city supposedly named Gorgoza in the Spaniard's honor. When Señor Gorgoza finally rode Young's Utah Central railroad after its completion in 1890, he was disappointed to find no memorial town at the end of the line. Nor would he ever recoup his investment.

Young's railroad was a source of contention among Mormon brethren at church headquarters and Young was finally persuaded to sell it to the Rio Grande Railroad Company, Union Pacific's competitor, in 1897. The rail was converted from narrow to standard gauge and carried freight and passengers between Salt Lake City and Park City until 1946. Zion's Bank occupies an out-building of the original depot.

Across the street from the Rio Grande Terminal, to your right, is a barn-like structure at 819 Park Avenue, the Kimball brothers' coal team barn. Next door, just past the gravel parking pad, is the little Kimball House.

15. Kimball House (817 Park Avenue)

This modest rectangular house was built by Burton T. Kimball in January 1882. Notice the saltbox slope to the rear roof. Burt's brother Edwin purchased a large tract of land here from Park City founder George Snyder for his and his brother's Coal Team Barn. Although Ed's principal occupation was mining supplies, he also served as one of the city's earliest mayors.

The Kimball Investment Company owned the 1885 four-square plan house next door at 811 Park Avenue and the dilapidated rectangular house on the corner. The latter was a double-celled dwelling—what passed as low-rent duplexes in early Utah.

Continue to Eighth Street. Turn right and walk west up the hill one short block to Woodside Avenue.

Turn right onto Woodside and proceed north past the old garage to your right. The first significant home you will encounter, third from the corner on your left, is painted blue, has white trim, and has a brown metal roof.

16. Raddon House (817 Woodside Avenue)

This sizeable bungalow has a distinctive south-side colonnade and sloping roof. It was built by LePage and Mae Raddon in 1916. LePage was the first-born son in Samuel Raddon Sr.'s second marriage to Louisa Harper and as such was heir to the *Park Record*. A partner with his uncle William A. Raddon beginning in 1924, LePage ran the *Record* until his death in 1956. Mae continued living here until 1978. The Raddons were next-door neighbors to another prominent Park City family in the gray, blue-trimmed crosswing cottage with the metal roof.

17. Smith Cottage (823 Woodside Avenue)

George W. Smith, a Mormon native of Wasatch County, moved to Park City in 1880, served as city treasurer, and was partner in the Smith and Brim meat shop on Main Street. Smith sold the house to Mormon bishop William Lewis when the bishop bought a Main Street dance hall in 1917. Two years later, where Deer Valley Drive intersects with Marsac Avenue, George vacillated between the two roads and at the last second turned uphill, rolling his automobile. George, his wife Mary, daughter, and sister were pinned inside the car. His son-in-law was thrown from the vehicle but managed to lift it off the other passengers. All survived except George who was crushed. The Raddons and Smiths faced feed yards on the other side of the street.

Proceed north. Brothers William and Roundy Smith, teamsters, lived in the yellow 1880s crosswing cottage to your left at 839 Woodside Avenue. Continuing north past the faint Ninth Street dirt lane, the 1885 crosswing cottage on your left at 905 Woodside is the historic home of Curtis Baldwin, a mine machinist, and his wife Pearl. Notice how its

Kimball House in foreground (Ill. 15)

Raddon House (III. 16)

south wall butts against the large Victorian house at 901. During the early twentieth century the right side of the street was filled with tenement housing. Two doors farther on the left was the residence of the unfortunate Wyckoff family. The front-yard decks are later additions.

18. Wyckoff Cottage (919 Woodside Avenue)

Jacob Wyckoff brought his family west to mine gold in Nevada and came to Park City in 1886 to work as a drayer, settling in this 1880s rectangular house altered into a crosswing cottage a short time after construction. After his wife's death in 1904, Jacob left the house to two of his children, Jacob and Bessie, while he moved in with his son-in-law and daughter Myra Gibson who lived nearby. Soon after resettlement, while his daughter languished from childbirth, Jacob suffered a fatal mining accident. Meanwhile Myra and her infant fared badly, went from bad to worse, and all three were buried in a triple-funeral.

Continue north past the new condominiums lining both sides of the street to the yellow T-house with brown trim on your left.

19. Meadowcraft Cottage (951 Woodside Avenue)

Charles Meadowcraft, a miner, built this crosswing cottage with the saltbox rear roof in 1886. William H. Dodge, early saloon keeper, bought it in 1890 and later sold to another saloon keeper, Thomas W. Clawson.

Next door, now an empty lot, is where Park City mercantilist Sherman Fargo and his wife Nellie lived between 1902 and 1927. Born in New York state in 1868, Sherman began his career in 1885 managing a branch of the Blyth-Fargo chain owned by his brother Lyman Fargo and Thomas Blyth. He began in Evanston, Wyoming, was transferred to Pocatello, Idaho, then assigned to Park City's store in 1902 which he supervised until it burned down in 1927.

Cross Tenth Street (unmarked), passing, on the northeast corner, an 1890 rectangular house with a saltbox roof and 1910 addition, nearly concealed by trees (1002 Woodside Avenue). The little green crosswing cottage next door, down a few steps from the street, is the Snyder Cottage.

20. Snyder Cottage (1010 Woodside Avenue)

Prominent mining official and attorney Wilson I. Snyder built here in the early 1880s. He lost his wife soon after from complications when a gangrenous limb was amputated. Wilson's uncle and aunt were Park City founders George and Rhoda Snyder who developed this neighborhood as Snyder's Addition. Wilson practiced law beginning at age twenty-two, later serving both as city and county attorney, grandmaster of the local International Order of Odd Fellows lodge, and president of the Utah Bar Association.

Although Wilson moved to Salt Lake City in 1901 to establish a new law partnership, his mining, legal, and real estate interests kept him bound to Park City. In 1910 he helped settle the long-standing Park City Townsite muddle by clearing land deeds buried in forty years of legal quagmire. He was an instructor in the University of Utah's School of Mines and served as vice-president of the Tintic Standard Mining Company.

Across the street to your left, one house to the north, is the Paull Cottage.

21. Paull Cottage (1013 Woodside Avenue)

This 1891 crosswing cottage was where Peter C. Paull, of the Main Street Paull Brothers' store, lived. His son Lawrence, a twenty-seven-year-old miner, was the first casualty of the flu epidemic of 1918-19.

John Flannagan, owner of the Main Street Cash Grocery, lived next door where there is now a vacant lot. To your right, notice the unnumbered off-white rectangular house with brown trim.

22. St. Jeor House (1020 Woodside Avenue)

W. D. "Tommy" St. Jeor lived in this circa 1905 rectangular house, though he was not the original owner. St. Jeor took up the job of city marshall in 1920 and was the bane of city bootleggers. The house has a north-side addition.

Next door, the cottage with the saltbox roof at 1026 Woodside was built in the 1880s. Across the street to your left is the Morgan dwelling, a gray cottage with white trim, built over a later garage addition.

23. Morgan Cottage (1027 Woodside Avenue)

Jesse Morgan moved this cottage here, possibly from the Burns lot three houses north, in 1889. Thirteen years later Jesse's estranged wife Nellie acquired ownership of the house. Jesse had been rooming with mining partner James Mazlin on Norfolk Avenue for several years. When Nellie left town four years later, she sold to Harry W. Wilson, a delivery driver for Blyth-Fargo, and his wife Gertrude. The Wilsons lived here with five children until the 1960s.

Continue past the green condominiums on your right. The large Victorian home on your left (1045 Woodside Avenue) stands on the site of frontier bartender James Burns's house. The crosswing cottage next door at 1053 Woodside began as an 1890 rectangular house. Around the turn of the century artist Willard Bircumshaw and wife May lived here. Next door is the Ridding House, painted gray with blue trim.

24. Ridding House (1057 Woodside Avenue)

Samuel B. and Mary Ridding were the first residents of this 1890s four-square. Samuel was a concentrator at the Silver King mill, meaning that he crushed ore-bearing rocks and loaded them into a machine which chemically bound silver ore. By concentrating close to mines, owners saved transportation costs to smelters where the ore was further purified.

Cross Eleventh Street to the north. The unnumbered corner house on your right is the Goodwin bungalow.

25. Goodwin House (1100 Woodside Avenue)

In 1928 William Scales, early Park City contractor and developer, built this and the bungalow next door at 1110 for physician Harold I. Goodwin. A Utah native, Goodwin was trained at the University of Utah and later worked at Holy Cross Hospital in Salt Lake City. Many of Park City's bungalows resemble the slightly earlier "pyramid" house. But this home is distinguished from the more classically-aligned four-square plan hybrids by the rectangular gable and the rectangular design of the façade's doors and windows. The porch is integrated with the rest of the house, framed with the same lap siding.

Across from the Goodwin House, on the corner at 1103 Woodside, is an 1892 rectangular house (now painted blue with white trim) with a cottage-making extension wing. Next door at 1107 Woodside is another 1890s cottage. Both were built by mill workers.

Continue north. The bluish-gray saltbox-roofed house on your right (1120 Woodside Avenue) is a late example of the simple rectangular plan (later expanded), constructed in 1906 for Finnish miner Charles Johnson and wife Agnes who took in laundry. In the 1890s James Archibald, a teamster, and wife Marie lived in the yellow cottage a few steps north on your left at 1127 Woodside.

Proceed to Twelfth Street (formerly known as Nelson Avenue), where the Carl Winters High School interrupts Woodside Avenue. Turn left to walk west up Twelfth Street one block.

Turn right onto Norfolk Avenue and continue north. The Innsbruck Family Chalet's office is to your left. Following Norfolk Avenue behind the school, you will pass the Skiers and Powder Ridge lodges to your left. Notice the view of Masonic Hill to the east where Masons performed ceremonies after their lodge burned down in 1898. Many modest mill workers' cottages once dotted this block.

At the corner of Norfolk Avenue and Thirteenth Street, on your left is one of the city's first ski lodges, built at the beginning of the modern tourist boom and located near the bottom of the first gondola ski lift.

26. Chateau Après Lodge and Cafe (1299 Norfolk Avenue)

The Chateau Après opened in 1964, the same year as Treasure

Mountain Inn. Ken Holt, the original owner, used to recruit young southern California women to work at the resort. The women were affectionately called Chateau Queens. Holt himself hailed from Santa Ana in Orange County, California, and leased the lot from the United Park City Mining Company.

Turn left at Thirteenth Street and ascend the wooden steps to Empire Avenue. To your right as you climb the stairs is The Shaft condominium complex.

At the top of the stairs, looking south down Empire Avenue, across the street to the west with Sweetwater inscribed on the north wall, is another of the town's first chateau-esque lodges, originally the C'est Bon. Clearly developers believed that upscale ski accommodations required French appellations. The original pseudo-French-Norman architecture was later remodeled by Sweetwater developers to resemble "an English country inn."

27. C'est Bon Hotel (1255 Empire Avenue)

This was the Park's first luxury hotel and convention center, completed in April 1970 for $750,000. It originally accommodated 200 guests and included three penthouse suites. In 1972, at the Western Governors' Conference held here, a Tacoma, Washington, journalist complained of the isolation from "real" nightlife in Salt Lake City. The C'est Bon lounge stripper, he complained, "takes her clothes off so fast, you get the idea she's getting ready for a skinny-dip and 'last one in is a rotten egg.'"

In 1978 the Sweetwater Company bought the C'est Bon and converted it into a timeshare condominium complex. Apparently the mock Tudor architecture befits the company name. Sweetwater took in an additional 50,000 square feet around the original 18,000-foot C'est Bon.

Turn right onto Empire Avenue and proceed north. At the corner of Manor Way, with the Acorn Chalet to your right, turn left and proceed one block west to Lowell Avenue. Here is the newest jewel in Park City's crown—not a silver mine but a ski resort. The Gables Hotel is directly in front of you.

28. The Resort Center and Park City Ski Area (1347 Lowell Avenue)

The Resort Center, completed in 1976, is a complex of seven multi-winged buildings with condominium hotel rooms, restaurants and clubs, boutiques, ski-rental shops, a gondola, and ticket offices. It serves as base camp for the Park City Ski Area which operates fourteen lifts, 89 runs and trails, five bowls, and a 23,000-skier-per-hour capacity. North America's World Cup skiing competition opens here each Thanksgiving weekend. In the summer the Pay Day lift takes adventurers to the Alpine Slide, a dual-track, half-mile-long run on a skateboard-like toboggan. Other summer activities include mountain biking on the Shadow Lake Loop and Sweeney Switchbacks trails, horse rentals, miniature golf, concerts, and dining.

The Resort Center represents Park City's phenomenal progress since the early 1960s when Summit County was officially designated a "depressed area." From its heyday when the town had thirty mines and a population of 11,000, Park City had dwindled to one mining concern employing a handful of men and a total population of 2,500. The nearest physician was twenty-five miles away in Kamas.

Most of the land in and around town (8,700 acres) was owned by the United Park City Mines Company (UPMC). A subsidiary, Treasure Mountain Resort Company, was created in the 1950s to transform the town into a ski haven to rival Snowmass, Colorado. Progress was slow, but the company constructed thirty-two steel towers in 1963 for the 2.5-mile Treasure Mountain Gondola Lift, North America's longest tramway.

The first phase in Treasure Mountain's master plan nearly sank the parent company, despite $1.2 million in federal loans. In 1970 Royal Street Development Company of Newport Beach, California, bought Treasure Mountain for $5.5 million with long-term leases for the slopes. Royal Street also bought the Mormon church's welfare ranch in Deer Valley and the 155-acre Snow Family ranch northwest of the resort. That summer the new Treasure Mountain Resort Company proceeded with a $100-million plan for chair lifts, a golf course, shops, homes, and condominiums.

In 1971 three lifts were completed: Pay Day, Crescent, and Lost Prospector. Six new runs were added, bringing the skier capacity to 7,000 per hour. Treasure Mountain scored a coup in October when it hired Olympic gold-medalist Stein Eriksen from the Snowmass, Colorado, ski school to be Park City's skiing director, bringing international attention to the resort. The *Park Record* noted at the end of 1971 that, whereas the mining company had invested $2 million in the resort over seven years, Royal Street had already spent $7 million in one year.

During the winter of 1972-73 the lifts worked at near capacity and Treasure Mountain was forced to impose use-limitations. It considered creating its own utilities district in light of Park City's limited water system, but the city subsequently brought its utilities capacity up to speed.

Royal Street investments reached $12.5 million by 1974. It constructed 132 condominiums, a restaurant and bar, commercial shops, and the U.S. Ski Team's headquarters at Mid-Mountain Lodge near the Silver King Mine site, halfway up the mountain above the resort complex. The ski team was lured here from Denver. Their offices were later moved to Park City's Main Street and then to Prospector Square.

Meanwhile UPMC passed hands twice: to an Anaconda Copper/Asarco Mining and Smelting partnership in 1970 and, after 1990, to Manhattan-based Loeb Investments, current owner of extensive private properties surrounding Park City.

In 1975 Alpine Meadows Company of Lake Tahoe, Nevada, headed by former BVD company president Nick Badami, purchased the Park City ski resort buildings and lease from Royal Street Resort. The latter retained Deer Valley.

Alpine Meadows implemented $7 million in improvements. The high-speed Eagle Quad Chair Lift replaced the old King Con triple lift which was moved. One run, named Clementine, was redesigned for World Cup races, and a giant slalom run, C.B.'s, was introduced, named after Craig Badami, vice-president and son of the resort president. Another change was random drug testing for employees, whereby management hoped to rein in the party-animal ski bums who flocked to work here. In response to employee complaints, management lauded Northwest Toxicology laboratory's service as the "pickiest in the country."

UPMC sued Park City and Deer Valley resorts in 1992 over alleged "fraud, racketeering, [and] conspiracy." The parties are still in litigation. In 1994 Salt Lake developer Ian Cumming's Powder Corporation purchased the resort from the Badamis in a $42 million deal. Cumming is former chair of the Utah Sports Authority.

Cross Lowell Avenue to the Resort Center. The first structure you encounter, The Gables Hotel, includes Moguls Espresso Cafe at the ground level.

29. The Gables Hotel (1335 Lowell Avenue)

Apart from the gondola and ticket office, the resort buildings represent a later phase of development. In 1980 Jack Davis, Snowflake Condominium developer, presented the city with an ambitious plan for "Park City Village": a vast complex of condominiums, lodging, retail sites, and parking facilities. Along with architects G. G. Schierle and Van Martin, Davis planned a non-European development that reflected more western American, Victorian influence. The complex of three-story buildings with steep, pitched roofs and dormers was thought to be particularly appropriate because it lacked the "massive look" of similarly sized structures and would blend nicely with already existing local buildings.

Proceed west along the stone walkway between The Gables and the south wing of the Resort Center Inn (The Chocolate Factory is at the ground level).

30. Resort Center Inn (1385 Lowell Avenue)

Proceed west up the walkway toward the tall brick building with the New England gothic steeple, the Silver Mill House. The popular Baja Cantina Restaurant occupies the visible ground level, open daily for lunch and dinner. The Inn reflects Jack Davis's architectural vision of low-key traditionally American resort styling.

31. Silver Mill House (1355 Lowell Avenue)

Park City Village did not receive final approval for construction until a year after its initial proposal to the city planning commission. Officials were worried about traffic tie-ups and wanted to institute mass transit in the city before the development was underway. So construction was divided into four phases. Commercial structures like this one were part of phases two and four, while residential and hotel buildings were given priority within phases one and three. The estimated $125 million project got off the ground in May 1981.

To your left are the Marsac Mill Manor Condominiums.

32. Marsac Mill Manor (1325 Lowell Avenue)

By 1983 construction of Park City Village Phase I buildings like this one was slowed down by a variety of problems including wrangling over height restrictions, run-away budgets, and contractor disputes. Prudential Financial Services Corporation, which backed Jack Davis, eventually exercised its option to acquire the development and opened up the condominiums to all real estate marketers while simplifying buying procedures. Construction resumed in summer 1984.

Prudential subsequently sued the former developer in 1986 for mishandling funds, faulty construction, and overcharges. The finance company also accused the architects of negligence, saying if they had known in 1983 of the defects, they would not have bought the development. Despite all of the setbacks, ski boosters saw the additional construction as imperative if Park City were to compete for international skiing tourism's dollars.

Ascend the stairs, past the Breeze Ski and Sport shop on your left, to the Main Plaza. The Gondola Building is straight ahead. Cross the plaza to the "Gondola" and "Cafeteria" signs.

33. Gondola Building (1315 Lowell Avenue)

The gondola runs to the top of 9,400-foot Pioneer Peak. It makes an intermediate stop at the Angle Station directly above the resort, then follows the ridge in a northwest direction to the end-station and Summit House Restaurant. In the building's north wing, upstairs, is Steeps Private Club. You can enter this sports bar by paying a minimal fee for a temporary membership.

From the "Gondola" and "Cafeteria" signs, proceed along the Main Plaza's west covered walkway, passing Gart Brothers Ski and Sports and The Cookie Bear on your left. Ahead to your right is the Village Loft with aisles leading to ticket windows.

Silver Mill House (III. 31)

34. Village Loft (1345 Lowell Avenue)

Angle to your left between the north wing of the Gondola Building (where there are public restrooms) and the Village Loft toward the Little Miners Park for children. From here you can see two ski runs and lifts: Pay Day, just past the children's carousel, which ascends the mountain in a southwestern direction; and Ski Team, west of the children's park at the tree line, which runs northwest. The Ski Team and Jupiter Bowl lifts were constructed in 1976 and opened 700 acres of expert ski terrain. The towers for the Jupiter Bowl lift, accessible from below Jupiter peak, were put in place by helicopter. Because the bowl has 80-degree grades and cannot be groomed, it is limited to serious skiers.

Walk to the breezeway entrance between the two wings of the Village Loft. There is an arrow-shaped "To Shops & Ice Rink" sign on the wall (and a sign pointing to "Kinderschule" hanging from the hallway rafters, though you should not follow this sign). Follow the breezeway to the stairs at the far end. You will pass The Eating Establishment Express, World Cup Ski Tuning, Village Gifts, and Destination Sports on your left, and the Race Department Office and Bootworks on your right.

Descend the stairs to the entrance of Shirt Off My Back II, the resort cousin to the the Main Street clothing store. Looking to your far left, you can see the Silver Putt Miniature Golf course and, above that, the Three Kings Ski Run and Lift.

Angle to your left past the Mountain Savior clothing store toward the Ziggy's Ristorante sign at the top of a flight of stairs. Walk down the stairs to the lower plaza and ice-skating rink. At the bottom, Ziggy's is on your left. Ahead to your right is the skating rink used as a dining patio in the summer. The two connecting wooden huts at the edge of the rink are an ATM center and a skate-rental booth. To your far left down the alley is the National Ability Center housing the Park City Handicapped Sports Association and Coyote Grill.

Angle to your left to the covered walkway of the Resort Center Lodge where Jan's Sports occupies the ground level. Owner Jan Peterson is a longtime Park City booster whose father owned Utah's first ski store in Salt Lake City's Sugarhouse district.

35. Resort Center Lodge and Inn (1415 Lowell Avenue)

This type of architecture is typified by massive, exposed structural members—timbers, reinforced concrete and steel, and shingled roofs. Decorative elements reference historic styles.

Proceed under the covered walkway of the Resort Center (with Jan's Sports to your left) to the short hallway between two wings of the Resort Center Lodge. Walk through the hallway to the stairs. KinderSport will be to your right and Ziegler & Associates Real Estate to your left.

Descend the stairs to the small patio landing. Across the parking lot to the east, the four-story red-brick building with the metal roof is the

Shadow Ridge Condominium Hotel, built on the original site of Miners Hospital. At the turn of the century this area was known as Nelson Hill.

At the far end of the patio landing is a metal stairway that descends to your left. Take these stairs to the Resort Center Lodge and Inn driveway, cross the driveway, and descend the few remaining steps to the parking lot.

Cross the parking lot diagonally (or hug the grassy edge to the north, then east, depending on traffic) to the intersection of Lowell Avenue and Silver King Drive, using caution taking this short-cut. The intersection you seek is bordered by cast-iron street lamps, a prominent stop sign, and a cement-and-wood marquee.

As you cross the parking lot, to your left you can see departure stations for the First Time Lift, heading up a gentle slope toward the southwest; the Three Kings Lift, heading southwest; and, against the base of the mountain behind an aspen grove, the new Eagle Lift heading straight up the mountain to the west. Utah governor Calvin Rampton cut the ribbon to open the 2,640-foot Three Kings chair lift in December 1970. It was named after the Three Kings Mine which operated until 1924. The Eagle Lift is for speed racing and competitive training.

At the intersection of Lowell Avenue and Silver King Drive, turn left and proceed west toward the mountains. You will pass a T-intersection with Three Kings Drive which winds its way toward Thayne's Canyon. The 96-unit Three Kings Condominium complex to your right was begun by Treasure Mountain in the summer of 1971. Units went for $30,000-$50,000 and nearly all were sold before construction was completed in December.

As you continue toward the end of Silver King Drive, passing the Snowflower Condominiums to your left, you can see the arched wrought-iron entrance to Glenwood Cemetery.

36. Glenwood Cemetery (Silver King Drive)

This memorial park was established in 1885 as an alternative to the city cemetery. Parkites felt that the sequestered trees and small creek provided a more pleasant resting place than the barren, windswept site near town. A fourth of the plat was reserved for members of fraternal orders and secret societies. Funeral arrangements were one of the benefits of belonging to Freemasonry or the International Order of Odd Fellows.

The plots are laid out within two looping paths, one to the northwest and the other to the southwest. At one time the hidden cemetery was threatened with extinction. Before residents banded together to ensure its protection, heavy machinery employed in nearby construction uprooted and crushed many of the headstones.

If you desire, you may pass through the iron gate (the walk-in entrance is to your right) placed in memory of Blanche Fletcher, an old-time resident and the last person buried here. As you stroll through the cemetery you will get a sense of the cultural and ethnic diversity of Park City, and may recognize several names of historic residents identified in this book. For example, one infamous grave belongs to Patrick Coughlin, executed in 1896 for slaying lawmen pursuing him for stealing strawberries from a fruit stand. His grave is at the far middle of the southwestern loop.

Retrace your steps from the cemetery back east along Silver King Drive beyond the intersection with Lowell Avenue to Empire Avenue. The Park City Municipal Golf Course is to your left. Park City became interested in the golf course when residents feared that it was going to be sold to developers and turned into more condominium complexes or a private country club. The city council re-zoned the area in 1979 but did not specifically define boundaries because the resort might have accused the city council of "stealing" their land. The city ended up paying around $1 million for the course to keep it public and undeveloped. It is an 18-hole, 6,700-yard course with more than the average amount of water.

Carefully cross Empire Avenue and continue east between the Snowcrest Hotel Condominium on your left and the Powderpointe Condominiums on your right, across Woodside Avenue to the convenience store on the far side of Park Avenue. The corner of Park and Empire is the site of the town's first traffic light in 1984.

Turn right and begin the short walk back to the Miners Hospital. Proceeding east, you will pass a red shiplap house with off-white trim and pyramid roof to your left at 1488 Park Avenue, a turquoise crosswing cottage at 1460, and a white crosswing cottage next door at 1450 Park Avenue.

Continue south, noticing the new pyramid-inspired house across the street to your right at 1373 Park Avenue. You will pass the Park Place Condominiums to your left and a little crosswing cottage to your right, followed immediately by Miners Hospital where you began. This ends the Lower Town and Park City Ski Resort walking tour.

BICYCLING TOURS

IV.
Snyderville Basin

DISTANCE: 10 MILES   TIME: 1.5 HOURS
DIFFICULTY: LOW

This tour follows State Road 224 (Park Avenue) from the Park City Municipal Golf Course to Kimball Junction and back. Parking is available at the golf course (1541 Thayne's Canyon Drive), which lies at the intersection of Park Avenue and Thayne's Canyon Drive. Look for the green-and-tan service station on the opposite side of the street. Adolph's restaurant, which shares parking with the golf course, specializes in Swiss cuisine and is open daily for dinner.

Begin by exiting the parking lot onto State Road 224. Turn left and head cautiously north in the bicycle lane that doubles here as an automobile turn lane. You will soon pass Prospector Drive on your left.

At the traffic signal—the intersection with Payday Drive/Holiday Ranch Loop Road—cross the road to the east toward the Radisson Inn and then continue north on the east side of 224. To your right you can see Park City's residential suburbs of Holiday Ranch, Willow Ranch, Ridgeview, and Park Meadows.

Continuing north, you will pass an intersection with Meadows Drive and encounter the picturesque Hurley Farm straddling the road on both sides. As you continue north, passing Quarry Mountain to the east, the road ascends a low hill and parallels McLeod Creek for a short distance. You are now on the outskirts of Park City in Summit County. After passing a tree farm to your left, you will see Snowed Inn Hotel and Juniper Restaurant on your right. The restaurant is open Thursday-Monday for dinner.

The ten-room Snowed Inn opened in 1986 when it was contructed as a replica of the Iowa farmhouse of one of the developer's great-grandmothers. The Inn features 10-foot ceilings, custom mahogany moldings, and a sunken bathtub in every room.

Following the road's long curve to the northeast, you will pass Parkwest Village. On your left is the entrance to the Wolf Mountain Ski Resort.

1. Wolf Mountain (4000 Park West Drive)

Park City West, as Wolf Mountain was first known, opened in 1968 with an old west theme. By 1969 Park West (as it was then known) had three lifts and a $1.5 million expansion plan. The next year the company added five new runs for a total of thirty miles of ski paths, including the Tumbleweed Run for beginners. The company acquired rights to 1,000

SNYDERVILLE BASIN

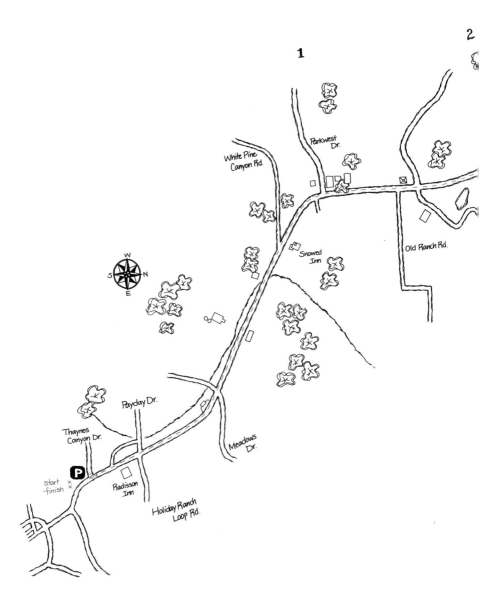

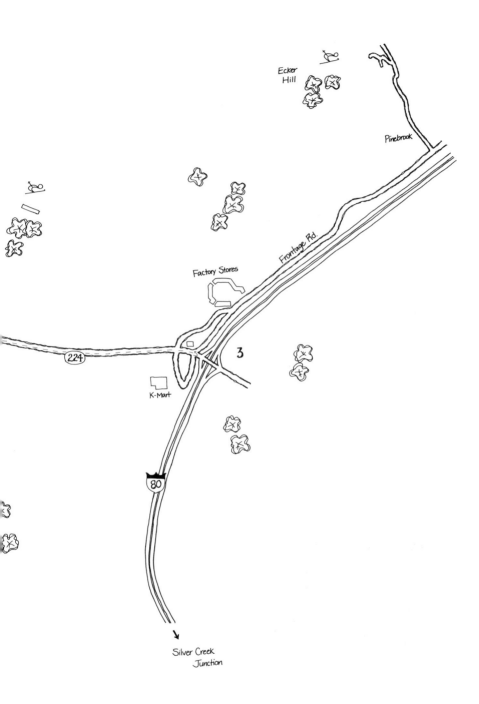

Ecker
Hill

Pinebrook

Frontage Rd.

Factory Stores

224

3

K-Mart

80

Silver Creek
Junction

Hurley Farm, State Road 224

acres on Jordanelle Reservoir, when the reservoir was still being planned. Park West's Jordanelle development, had it materialized, would have included residential lots, a marina, a golf course, and convention facilities.

But Park West was plagued by management conflicts. In 1971 Life Resources, Inc., a San Bernardino, California, recreational development company, acquired 80 percent of the resort's stock. Ford Motor Company financed a condominium development in 1974, but the mid-1970s recession drove developers into bankruptcy and the complex became a ghost town. In 1976 Ford transferred the condominium property to a Los Angeles attorney, while Park West unsuccessfully sued Park City Ski Resort for influence peddling with the city council.

In 1982 much-needed capital surfaced from White Pine Management Corporation and, five years later, from investor Jack Giloman, owner of the Riverhorse and Barking Frog restaurants in Park City. Finally in 1993 Kenneth Griswold and Annette and Michael Baker purchased the resort and held a promotional contest to rename it. They liked Wolf Mountain because of the endangered species reference, which created "an educational environment that raised awareness." In the same spirit ski runs were renamed in honor of wombats and salamanders, a change from previous cowboy-and-Indian designations.

During the 1990s downhill skiing lost popularity nationwide while its cousin, snowboarding, became the fastest growing winter sport in the country. Park City and Deer Valley ignored the fad, while Wolf Mountain embraced it, installing a day-and-night snowboard run. Holly Flanders, two-time Olympian and former skiing director at the Park City Ski Resort, joined Wolf Mountain as head of ski operations, and five new intermediate trails were created.

Wolf Mountain has also become popular as a summer outdoor concert venue. An indoor auditorium recently opened to allow for winter concerts as well. Although crowds in excess of 15,000 engender local complaints about traffic, noise, and crime, most people don't seem to mind the mixing of music and nature.

Continue north, passing Miss Billie's Kids Kampus and summer camp and the Snyder's Mill development on your right. As you begin a slow descent along State Road 224, the expansive Snyderville Basin opens before you on the right. This is the latest—but certainly not the last—battleground for property development in the area. A relatively flat basin with freeway access for a short commute to Salt Lake City, Snyderville Basin has been eyed by developers for some time. It is an environmentally sensitive area with limited water resources and is potentially subject to wintertime pollution inversions.

At Old Ranch Road is a Snyder's Mill development sign, named for the sawmill built by Samuel Snyder in 1853. Snyder purchased property rights from Mormon apostle Parley P. Pratt, who used the meadows nearby here for keeping livestock, hence the name Parley's Park. A tiny community grew up around the mill in the 1860s to become Snyderville. Beyond that, at the intersection with Bear Hollow Drive/Silver Spring Drive, is a large residential development on either side of State Road 224 known as Canyon Rim Village. To your right, notice Parley's Park Elementary School. This area was developed beginning in 1970 by Salt Lake City-based Terracor on land once used by local Mormons to grow food for the poor. The residences were designed by Salt Lake City architect Ronald Molen.

On the left is the entrance to the Utah Winter Sports Park.

2. Utah Winter Sports Park (3000 Bear Hollow Drive)

This area was first occupied by William O. Anderson, a polygamist. Anderson built a home where the Welcome Inn now stands for his second wife Elsie. During the winter of 1875 Anderson left Elsie to visit his other wife in Kamas, became lost in a blizzard, and in the absence of an available doctor, had parts of his frostbitten feet amputated by neighbors. Meanwhile Elsie gave birth to twins, only one of whom survived. The other was left in a milkhouse until a grave could be dug when the ground thawed.

Bear Hollow is now home to the $7.2 million Olympic sports park. In 1992 Utah residents passed a resolution allowing the state to loan $42 million to the Salt Lake City Olympic Bid Committee for construction of facilities. Although Utah lost the 1998 bid to Nagano, Japan, the state later won the international nod for the 2002 Winter Olympic Games. The local Olympic committee is private and manages the facilities on its own. The Bear Hollow installation includes Nordic and Freestyle ski-jumps, a luge run, a double chairlift, handle tow, and summer jumping facilities. The public is invited to watch as the U.S. Ski Team trains. When the runs are not occupied, the public can test the jumps themselves under supervision.

Continue north as the road now snakes northwest, then northeast. Of all development in this area, this road itself is one of the longest-running and most controversial additions to the valley. Work on expanding the two-lane state road began in the early 1970s just as the city's ski boom hit. Adequate transportation was necessary for the ski industry, but as in other areas residents were of two minds about this expansion. Contractors proposed sending the road underground to minimize the impact. Local officials finally decided to purchase corridors of land as buffer areas to create a parkway for commuter enjoyment.

You will pass the Northshore Estates, Ranch Place, and Cutter Lane to your right, followed by the B-D Ranch.

By now you can see the Golden Arches at Kimball Junction, the intersection with Interstate 80. Stop at Frontage Road.

3. Kimball Junction

The area where the two highways connect (224 and 80) is called Kimball Junction after stage coach driver William H. Kimball. Originally the Mormon Trail passed by here and veered off just below Parley's Summit (named after Mormon pioneer Parley Pratt) to follow Emigration Canyon down into the Salt Lake Valley. Pratt built a tollroad here and earned $1,500 in 1850 from gold prospectors en route to California.

To your far right, on the north side of Interstate 80, is the Silver Creek Estates community at Silver Creek Junction where I-80 meets U.S. Route 40. Many of these developments began in the late-70s when they began the laborious passage through the county's planning commission. Fortunately, a sizable area of the land bordering highways 224 and I-80 has been preserved through the beneficence of the late Leland Swaner and his family who set aside much of it as Swaner Memorial Park. To your immediate right, the K-Mart built in 1992 encountered considerable protest. Local environmentalist and sometime political candidate Todd Gabler chained himself to the construction equipment, was arrested, and fined $350 for criminal trespass. Gabler claimed that more construction would deplete the Snyderville Basin drainage area and contribute to air pollution.

To your left, not far from here on Frontage Road/Landmark Drive, is the popular Factory Stores at Park City with fifty manufacturer's outlets. Beyond that, the Pinebrook development, organized in the late 1970s, surrounds the Ecker Hill ski-jump ruins, named for Peter Ecker, early Utah Ski Club president. Built in 1930, Ecker Hill was a world-class ski jump where Alf Engen broke five world records and the 1949 national championships were held. Now only a few splintered timbers remain of the tower and platform. The site was listed on the National Register of Historic Places in 1986. Farther down Frontage Road are the remains of an early chair lift. The Pinebrook residential area was developed in the early 1970s when Meeks Wirthlin and Edwin Vetter subdivided their Gorgoza Pines Ranch. Gorgoza was a Spanish aristocrat whom John Young, son of Brigham Young, recruited to fund a railroad from Salt Lake City to Park City. Young flattered the wealthy Spaniard with maps of a non-existent town named Gorgoza, without mentioning that the town was contingent upon the railroad's success.

Cross to the west side of State Road 224 and begin the return trip south. You will find the scenery even more impressive on the ride back, facing the mountains as opposed to riding away from them. Notice the Olympic park ski jump in the foothills ahead of you to the west.

Continuing south, you will pass a horse ranch on your right, then pursue a gradual climb toward the entrance to the Utah Winter Sports Park. After the Park City Nursery you will come upon a historic four-square house with a front-center dormer and porch gable with decorative posts.

Pedaling farther south, and climbing gradually, you will pass an

Ecker Hill ski jump ruins

Olympic Park ski jump

old red barn and newer blue bungalow partially concealed by trees (4137 State Road 224) and a church. After the church, a convenience store is located just inside the entrance to Wolf Mountain.

Cross Park West Drive and follow the curve to the southeast. Approaching Park City, White Pine Canyon Road intersects the road to your right, followed by a rest stop, a ranch, and The Homestead residential development. Notice the view of Park City Ski Resort, upper Park City, and Deer Valley ahead of you. More immediately, you can now see the Radisson Inn at the Payday Drive/Holiday Ranch Loop Road intersection.

Cross the intersection to the south and continue past Prospector Drive to the golf course parking lot. This ends the Snyderville Basin bicycle tour.

V.
Empire Canyon

DISTANCE: 8 MILES   TIME: 2 HOURS
DIFFICULTY: MODERATE

This tour takes you south on Daly Avenue, up Empire Canyon to the Daly Mine ruins, and back along Ontario Ridge to historic Prospect Avenue. From there it is a short ride back to where you began. Those with mountain bikes will appreciate the narrow, steep descent from the ridge, while those with street bikes may prefer to walk that portion of the trail.

Parking is available at the public lot south of the Wasatch Brew Pub at the head of Main Street (250 Main Street). It is accessible from Swede Alley.

Cycle south on Main Street, angling to the southwest, to the turn-around where Main Street becomes Daly Avenue. There is a yellow "Dead End" sign and a blue "Residential Area" arrow at the street's entrance.

Daly Avenue through lower Empire Canyon was the primary route to the city's first mines, as well as the earliest and most thickly settled of the city's canyon "suburbs." For the Park's first half-century this road was little more than a dirt trail leading to the Judge Mine. The houses were popular among Johnny-Come-Lately miners from eastern and southern Europe who began replacing northern European labor forces in the 1890s and early 1900s. The old Ontario boarding house at 176 Prospect Avenue on Ontario Ridge, the hill south of Daly Avenue, closed around 1910. Many of the Slavic miners, called "Bohunks," consequently moved into miners' cottages on lower Daly Avenue. For that reason residents nicknamed the road "Bohunk Alley."

Proceed south on Daly Avenue, passing four matching Empire Canyon condominium structures on your right, to the three-story de Grover house sitting above the street at the top of a steep wooden staircase.

1. de Grover House (68 Daly Avenue)

Nom Quon Low de Grover owned numerous turn-of-the-century cafes, lodging houses, and rental properties. This large 1880s house, his private residence, was bequeathed along with his other holdings to his son Joe and later sold to the Christian Berriocha family, 1890 German immigrants and miners. Notice the cut-away balcony on the first level, the saltbox slope of the roof in back, and the angled corners.

Continue one-half block farther south, just past the two old,

EMPIRE CANYON

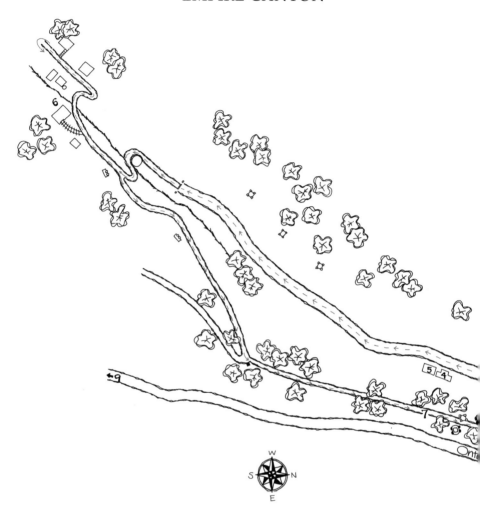

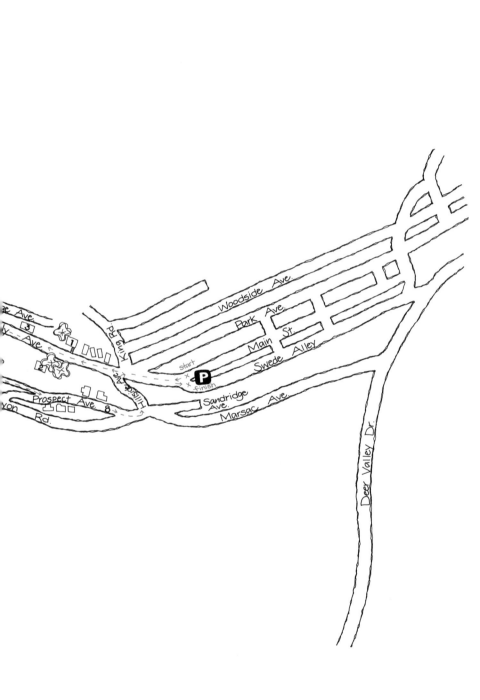

wooden, single-cell garages on your left. Recessed from the street and nearly concealed by trees is the Mahoney Cottage.

2. Mahoney Cottage (97 Daly Avenue)

Miner Bart and Josie Mahoney, Irish emigrants, adapted this hall/parlor house to a crosswing cottage with a northern addition. One of the ways to discern an altered rectangular house is by examining the arrangement of openings on the stem-wing. Instead of one door and one window in assymetrical fashion, crosswing cottages-by-addition betray their humble origins by the symmetrical tripartite arrangement of one door and two windows on the stem-wing. This circa 1880 rectangular house was added to ten years later. Marcella K. Taylor Smith purchased the house in 1917 and lived here nearly sixty years. Be sure to notice the little wooden footbridge leading to the house across the dry creek bed.

For the city's first half-century Daly Avenue miners built cottages primarily on the east side of the street, across Silver Creek, with their backs butted up against Ontario Ridge. The creek now runs under the street, which you may notice when you pass an occasional gutter drain and hear the creek rushing below. Approximately thirty historic cottages still dot this quaint avenue, most set back against the hill on the east side.

Ride up the street another half-block to the white, blue, and pink Frkovich crosswing cottage, this time on your right. Notice the storage areas built into the retaining wall and foundation.

3. Frkovich Cottage (162 Daly Avenue)

Mike Frkovich built this house in the 1880s and lived here into the 1920s. Among Frkovich's slavic neighbors was Mike Bayer Umiljenovic across the street in the 1890s four-square plan structure at 145 Daly. Umiljenovic bought the house after John Ledingham, the previous owner, died of miner's consumption in 1917. During Prohibition, as police regularly raided stills hidden behind Daly residences and up the canyon's side, the *Park Record* noted with its usual bite: "Look at the names of those arrested. There is nothing American about it, so why should leniency be extended?" Police conducted a boarding house raid on Daly Avenue and arrested one man who was pimping for his wife, adding to the street's reputation as one of the city's seedier neighborhoods.

Continue up Daly, past the intersection with Ridge Avenue on your right, to the white crosswing cottage with a metal roof, fronted by a wooden and metal barn, on your left. The house sat in front of the creek which snaked back toward the ridge at this point, according to turn-of-the-century Sanborn insurance maps.

4. Norbirath Cottage (291 Daly Avenue)

Consturction of this house was probably begun around 1890, but the first known owner was Clement Norbirath, a German partner with A. R. Houstein in the early twentieth-century Summit Meat and Grocery store. Norbirath moved to Washington state in 1922.

Immediately next door is the McDonald House.

5. McDonald House (297 Daly Avenue)

This frame hall/parlor house was built around 1885 by J. R. and Alice McDonald, later occupied by Joseph C. McDonald, their son. The front wing is original, while the rear extension was added by 1900. Later residents were Nick Borovich, Nick Marovich, and Jack Busio—all Slav/Croat emigrants. Busio added a larger rear extension in 1929 to accommodate his large family and Slavic boarders. Their neighbors included John and George Tengo, Tyrolian mining brothers; Croatians Joseph and Annie Butkavitch who opened a "pool hall" on Main Street; and Peter and Annie Drokovich who operated one of several Croatian boarding houses.

Continue up Daly Avenue along Silver Creek, which you will see is still above ground at this elevation. After about a half-mile the pavement ends at a gate with a "No Trespassing" sign, a bicycle path around to the left, and a "Tour des Suds Trail/Mountain Trails Adopt a Trail Program" sign.

Proceed around the gate and continue south. The grade is steep for a short stretch as you approach a large city water tank to your left.

Ride past the water tank, then cross over the creek to the left. Take the switchback and continue south on the east side of Silver Creek. It is an easy ride to the old mine.

6. Judge Mining and Smelting Company Ruins (Empire Canyon)

As you approach the mine, the first structure you will encounter is an aging storage shed to your left, followed by the remains of a narrow-gauge railway, the mine entrance, and a company office building with a still-intact safe and fire-hose outlets. The principal mining claims were approximately a half-mile farther up the mountain.

To your right, across the creek and drain tunnel with water cascading into the creek, is a path that leads to the rest of the mine ruins. Follow the path toward the electrical relay station and turn left. Here you will see an old shed that housed machinery for the electric tramway that carried workers and ore from mid-town to the mine entrance, a laboratory full of drilling-core samples, a drain tunnel valve shed, an old elevator house for unloading ore, and a filtration area.

Return to the mine entrance at the lower area. Originally this was a Judge Drain Tunnel adit, built when miners struck an underground water source in 1896 and the mine flooded. John J. Daly, formerly a

Judge Mining and Smelting Company ruins (V. 6)

Judge Mining and Smelting Company ruins (V. 6)

schoolmaster, built the tunnel to drain his silver and zinc mine shafts southwest of here. He purchased the site in 1891. Two years later he brought in Robert Chambers, an investor, as vice-president of the reorganized Daly-West Company and was rumored to have capital from Ali Ben Haggin, an Arab capitalist who financed the famous Anaconda Copper mine near Butte, Montana.

Daly's fortunes were good until the mine flooded. The neighboring Ontario Mine's drain tunnel could have resolved his problem, but he could not induce the company to assist him. So he bid on a contract to dig a drain tunnel for Edward Ferry's Anchor Mine, of which the Judge Tunnel is a part. The Anchor was in trouble because of its large capital investments, Edward Ferry's 1901 illness, and partner David McLaughlin's death the same year. Daly took advantage of the situation and acquired through litigation the Anchor Mine and drain tunnel.

Daly sold George Hearst's interest in Daly-West to Salt Lake City capitalist Simon Bamberger and then acquired the Bonanza flat claims of John Judge's widow. After Robert Chambers's death in 1901, the Bambergers independently acquired the Ontario mines and Snake Creek claims. Then the Daly-Judge Mining Company faced tragedy. An explosion at the No. 2 shaft set off a chain reaction which led to the deaths of thirty-four miners in both the Daly-Judge and Ontario mines which were connected underground. Daly's failing health compelled him to turn over the company's presidency to the Bambergers the following year. Then in 1913 the Daly-Judge company's mill at this site burned to the ground. It built a new mill and smelter in Deer Valley.

After a series of bonanzas and tragedies, lawsuits and claim sales, George Lambourne, who had risen from a Daly miner to superintendent and finally controlling stockholder, reorganized all of the Daly properties into first the Judge Mining and Smelting Company (JM&S Co.) in 1918 and then, with additional acquisitions, as the Park City Mining and Smelting Company four years later. This mill site was constructed during the JM&S Co.'s brief reign. By the mid-1920s the entire eastern region was brought together under the reorganized Park Utah Consolidated Mining Company. The former Judge Mining and Smelting Company site was abandoned in 1952.

Take the path that brought you to the mine back toward Park City a short distance (without descending to the water tank) and turn right to follow the switchbacks up to the top of Ontario Ridge. Midway to the top be sure to notice, to the right of the path, the rail cars that once carried ore through the Daly mine tunnels. Across Empire Canyon, where the mountain is scarred, you can see the old tram towers leading to the mine. Rusted and decaying, they resemble ski lift towers.

Continue north through the remains of a gate to the top, then farther north toward the blue dumpster with a yellow pole to its side. Veer to the left of the pole and proceed down the narrow bicycle trail that follows the edge of the ridge. (If you have not turned soon enough, you will see a cluster of yellow- and blue-roofed industrial buildings across Ontario Canyon, meaning that you have gone too far.)

Keep to this main bicycle trail which descends steeply, with Empire Canyon to your left and Ontario Canyon to your right. This ridge was once dominated by the famous Ontario mine and mill.

7. Ontario Ridge

Though little is left of the Ontario quarry, it was Park City's preeminent silver mine for decades. Discovered by prospectors in 1872 and purchased by California capitalist George Hearst the same year, it added to the Hearst fortune which included previous interests in Virginia City, Nevada's Comstock Lode. Son William Randolph Hearst is known as the inventor of American yellow journalism and the inspiration for Orson Welles's classic movie *Citizen Kane*. One of the prospectors who discovered the ore deposits was named James Kane.

George Hearst placed Robert Chambers in charge of operations at the Ontario Mine. Eventually it was expanded to include a mill, constructed in 1877 with forty stamps to form bars of ore, or ingots, bearing at times the company's insignia.

Throughout its history the Ontario Mine was plagued by flooding. A huge 500-ton Cornish pump was installed that eliminated 2,500 gallons per minute, and eventually an enormous three-and-a-half-mile drain tunnel had to be dug from here to the Jordanelle Valley. The tunnel was said to be haunted by "whitecaps," supernatural entities that miners believed inhabited these subterranean labyrinths. One miner, Hugh Crawford, attempted suicide to escape Ontario whitecaps and later escaped from a Salt Lake City hospital to run naked through city streets. It is not surprising that miners developed such superstitions. The tunnels stank of human excretion, rotting timber, stagnant water, and blasting powder. Temperatures rose as the depth increased, and dim candlelight or bared bulbs barely penetrated the gloom of pervasive dust.

In 1907 an economic depression, followed by a drain tunnel cave-in, signaled the beginning of a slow demise for the Ontario Mine. In 1925, after being incorporated into the Park City Consolidated Mining Company, it experienced a ten-year heyday but later fell victim to unsteady metal markets and labor disputes.

Continuing along the dirt trail, you will pass another interesting feature of the ridge: the ruins of old houses and mid-century automobiles (a Packard, a Chevrolet, and a suicide-door Chrysler), just after another old tram tower. The rectangular houses were once part of an extended Prospect Avenue which was originally a simple, single-lane trail. When you exit the dirt trail, pause a moment on the paved portion of Prospect Avenue to enjoy the view. Since the grade just after this point is steep, stopping intermittently is difficult. You may want to read about

View from Ontario Ridge (V. 7)

the street's history here before braving this slope. Many of the houses on this block date from before the turn of the twentieth century.

8. Prospect Avenue

Unlike "Bohunk" Avenue, Prospect was a mixed neighborhood ethnically and otherwise. Domestic partners Peter Jansen and Frank Blacklin were Lithuanian miners who emigrated around 1902 and lived here through the 1920s. Their neighbors included Swedish miner Adolph Johnson and wife Frieda, with six children; single Irish miner Adolph O'Lachley; Scottish mining couple John M. and Janet McDougall; and a boarding house for bachelors.

Among the many still-existing structures is the blue-and-white crosswing cottage on the east side of the street (59 Prospect Avenue), built in the 1890s by Andrew and Julia A. Welch. It was bought about 1899 by Frederick W. Sherman, superintendent of the Daly West Mine, and his wife Lizzie. Sherman studied mining at Oberlin College, then came west as a fur trader, and eventually received numerous patents for his mining inventions. After Lizzie died in 1913, he left for Arizona and John C. Thompson took over both the superintendent's job and the house.

The multi-colored, multi-styled house next door (57 Prospect Avenue) with the interesting Italianate front bay was built in 1891 by Joseph J. and Sarah J. Jenkins who moved here from the Nevada Comstock Mine that year. Four years later Joseph moved to Salt Lake City and died of miner's consumption.

Next door, the yellow-and-white cottage (51 Prospect Avenue) was constructed in the 1880s by John and Esther Lindsay. Thomas H. Paull, who ran a Main Street hardware and grocery business, lived here in the 1930s.

On the west side of the street (36 Prospect Avenue) is a blue-and-white crosswing cottage built by English emigrants Richard and Annie Barrett about 1882. They had married in Virginia City and decided to settle here with their four children. On Park City's steep hillsides, conventional rear house-expansions were difficult, so cottages like this often received unusual side-wings and front additions.

The cottage two doors away (22 Prospect Avenue) was constructed around 1885 by Joseph Durkin. Originally T-shaped, it was subsequently modified into an "L" in 1907. Durkin worked for the Ontario Mine but later became a member of the city council. Durkin's neighbors included the secretary of Miners Hospital, Andrew Long, and Finnish emigrant Gus Carlson who owned one of the notorious Prohibition-era pool halls on Main Street.

Proceed carefully straight ahead down Prospect Avenue to the intersection with Hillside Avenue to your left. To your right is Marsac Avenue/Ontario Canyon Road which becomes Guardsman Pass Road farther south. Pause briefly.

9. Guardsman Pass Road

In the 1950s Park City officials petitioned the state to build a road over Guardsman Pass, hoping to lure people skiing in Brighton and Solitude resorts up Big Cottonwood Canyon to spend some time across the mountain in Park City. The unpaved drive offers stunning mountain and valley vistas, navigable during summer months in a sturdy, four-wheel drive vehicle.

Turn left onto Hillside Avenue. Follow it past Sandridge Avenue as it doubles back down the hill to the turn-around.

At the intersection with Daly Avenue, turn right onto Main Street and follow it one block northeast to the Wasatch Brew Pub parking lot where you began. This ends the Empire Canyon bicycle tour.

VI.
Telemark Hollow

DISTANCE: 15 MILES   TIME: 3.5 HOURS
DIFFICULTY: HIGH

This tour, which begins at Prospector Square Parking Lot G, takes you east on a "Rails-to-Trails" path that parallels Kearns Avenue, then south along the west shore of the Jordanelle Reservoir, west on Heber Avenue through Telemark Hollow to McKinley Gap, down into Deer Valley, and back to Prospector Square.

If you are unaccustomed to a moderate amount of daily exercise, this tour may not be for you. The first half is mostly downhill, but you may choose to walk your bicycle up Telemark Hollow. From the gap you can coast most of the way back. Be sure to take something to drink and protection from the sun. If the weather is unsettled, or if it has just rained, you may want to wait for a better day.

To reach Prospector Square Parking Lot G, head east on Kearns Boulevard (State Road 248) from Park Avenue. You will pass the Yarrow Hotel and Village Holiday Center on your right and the Park City Cemetery on your left. At the traffic light, just after the "Rail Trail" sign, turn right onto Bonanza Drive and then immediately left onto Prospector Avenue. Parking Lot G is on the right between the Associated Title Company building and the Sun Creek Condominiums. At the south end of the lot is a small gazebo topped by a "Park City" sign. To the left of the gazebo is a "Rail Trail Parking" sign and a dirt ramp to the trail.

1. Prospector Square

Despite its quaint name, Prospector Square is a modern multi-block commercial district developed in the mid-1970s by Donald H. Panushka & Associates, the same Salt Lake City architects who designed the principal Park City Ski Resort structures in the 1960s. A famous co-investor was Hollywood actor Henry Winkler who played "The Fonz" on the television sitcom *Happy Days*. The original intent was to "recapture the design flavor of Park City in its mining heyday," but the result was a largely monotone office-building complex with a nod to Alpine resort style in dark wood trims.

The development has attracted popular condominium hotels, restaurants such as Off-Main Cafe Bakery and Nacho Mamma's, and specialty shops such as A Woman's Place Bookstore. The Chamber of Commerce is located here as are the *Park Record* building, a state liquor store, and a Planned Parenthood office. The latter replaced a late-1970s

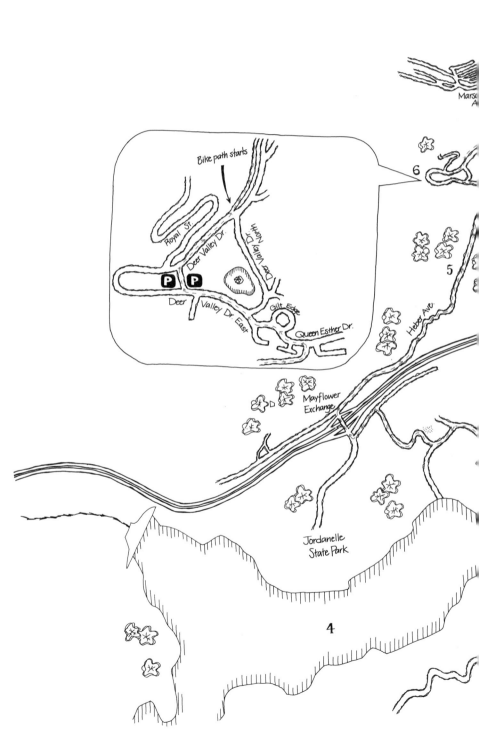

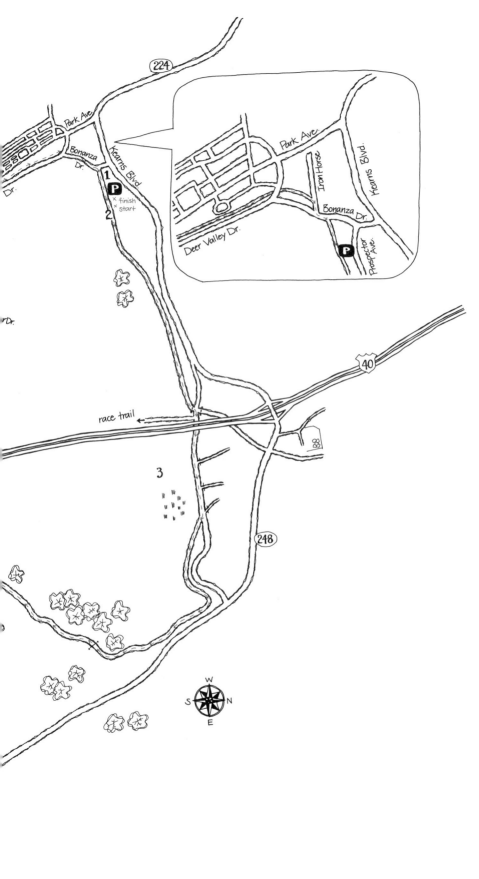

public clinic which the County Health Board opposed because, as they said, it served local "transients" and "Spanish People." Ironically the forced closing led to the opening of a private clinic over which the county has little control.

Prospector Square stretches from Bonanza Drive on the west to Gold Dust Lane on the east, from Kearns Boulevard on the north to Prospector Avenue on the south. It is complemented by Prospector Village residential development and Prospector Park, both farther east.

2. Rails-to-Trails

The idea of turning old railroad beds into bicycle and foot paths was introduced here in 1988, copying successful conversions in other western states. The national Rails-to-Trails Conservancy Group took advantage of the federal Rail Banking Act that granted right-of-way to unused railroads contingent upon future mass transportation needs. Labor and machinery were provided by the Utah National Guard and local businesses to transform the old Union Pacific beds entering Park City from the east. Removal of railroad ties left the surface bumpy, requiring grading and paving, and toxic mine tailings between the square and U.S. Interstate 40 required six inches of topsoil. For years tailings from neighboring mines had been dumped along the rails wherever room allowed. The Rails-to-Trails route officially opened on 3 October 1992.

Ascend the dirt ramp to the Rail Trail and turn left to proceed east along the side of Silver Creek. As you can see from the mileage sign, the trail is extensive, though this tour follows the trail for a short distance. Be sure to follow the main path and not veer off onto a side route.

As you proceed east, notice the tennis courts at the Prospector Athletic Club to your left. The club is surrounded by ten matching buildings, comprising The Inn at Prospector Square, followed by the Prospector Village residential area. The upscale homes in this neighborhood have prominent Victorian motifs. Builders were required to replicate existing Park City architecture and dutifully added cupolas, gingerbread trim, and octagonal towers to otherwise standard suburban architectural designs.

Toward the end of the residential area, cross Wyatt Earp Way and continue east. You will pass a 1-mile marker and cross two short wooden bridges. State Road 248 is to your left. You will soon see U.S. Interstate 40 to the east.

Continue on the bicycle path until it intersects with an asphalt frontage road. There is a gate here that you can ride through and just past the gate railroad tracks embedded in the road.

Turn right onto the road and proceed southeast. (Don't continue through the second gate; if you pass a 2-mile marker you have gone about fifty feet the wrong way.) You will climb briefly toward a freeway overpass. To your right, shortly before the highway overpass, the dirt trail that converges with the road is the starting point for one of the Park City Chamber of Commerce's designated bike paths and for National

Offroad Bicycle Association race trials. This was also site of the 1991 World Cup Race. The terrain here is steep and difficult.

Continue under the overpass where the pavement gives way gradually to gravel and areas of asphalt. Follow the trail as it gently curves toward State Road 248. This area is known as Richardson Flat.

3. Richardson Flat

In 1993 the Environmental Protection Administration considered putting the flat on its superfund clean-up list because of Keetley Mine tailings dumped here by the United Park City Mine Company. Tailings are metallic, highly-toxic refuse from mine workings: the garbage ores.

As you continue riding, now parallel to State Road 248 though some distance from it, notice the heavy industrial activity about half-mile to your left, across U.S. Interstate 40 near its junction with State Road 248. This was the Harper construction company's facility. Harper was the main contractor in expanding State Road 224 which comes into town from the south and bypasses the Wolf Mountain and Park City ski resorts, eventually becoming Park Avenue.

Park City officials authorized Harper to build an amphitheater for Shakespearean productions at the junction of the highways and halted construction in 1992 when Harper used its permit to assemble an industrial rock-crushing unit there instead. Still no theater, rock-crushing has resumed under the name Monroc. In addition to the State Road 224 project, Harper provided gravel for the Winter Sports Park near Snyderville.

Continuing east, you will pass two gated roads on your left that connect with the main path. Stay on the main road until the intersection with a third road, just after the swampy pond to your right. This is the old bed of the Union Pacific Railroad spur line which once served the Keetley Mine. It crosses your path diagonally. (You will notice a small hill in the main road in front of you. If you begin to climb a hill, you have gone too far.)

Turn right—riding parallel to the power lines—to follow the gravel path and discover the ingenuity of converting railbeds for recreational traffic. Though the terrain is steep, the Rail-Trail provides a gradual incline over ravines and through hills.

Continue along the railbed, ignoring side trails, in a gentle curve to the southeast. You will notice an occasional iron spike, rail fragment, or tie splinter along the way. At the clearing where a section of the rail is still visible, with an eroding cement foundation to your right and a gate to State Road 248 to your left, continue straight ahead where the path becomes less developed.

You will soon encounter a gate and a bike path around to the left. Stay on the trail for the next few hundred yards. Utah's 1979 Landowner Liability Act encouraged owners to open private land to public access, but passage through does not imply free range.

The trail winds to the southwest along a steady downhill slope.

Besides the immediate mountain scenery, you will be treated to a spectacular view of the Jordanelle Reservoir.

4. Jordanelle Reservoir

Settlement of the southern end of this valley began in the 1860s as residents of Heber City moved north. Far to the south the Federal Bureau of Land Management began constructing a dam in the 1960s where the Provo River flows through the Jordanelle Narrows. When the reservoir was first filled in 1993, it flooded the villages of Hailstone and Keetley. Notice how the old stretch of U.S. Interstate 40 now leads straight into the water. Across the reservoir you can see the Hailstone Marina, part of the new Jordanelle State Park.

As you continue descending into the valley, notice the ski runs on 9,400-foot Bald Mountain ahead of you to the southwest. Eventually you will approach a gravel pit. Follow the intersecting road which heads down to the left, then make an immediate right up the paved incline along the side of the pit. You will see a wooden retaining wall to your right, followed by the remains of an early rail, a small pond, and gravel company structures.

Follow the paved road as it makes three south-to-west bends away from the gravel pit. It's a bit steeper here than it appears. You will be surprised to look back and see your vertical progress.

At the T-intersection with the frontage road parallel to U.S. Interstate 40, turn left and ride up the hill to the T-intersection with the road that leads down to the reservoir and Jordanelle State Park. Take a minute to look to your right across U.S. Interstate 40 to the southern foothills where you can see the roofs of the abandoned Mayflower Mining community.

Turn right toward U.S. Interstate 40's Mayflower Exchange, named after the mine and the Dutch company that developed this end of the Jordanelle shoreline. Carefully ride across the overpass, watching for traffic both entering and leaving the highway.

After crossing the highway, turn right onto unpaved Heber Avenue, once the main stage road between Park City and Heber City. Follow the road north, parallel to U.S. Interstate 40. It then curves west, away from the highway, where you will soon encounter a rustic "Heber Avenue" sign. Continue following the main trail as it climbs north, then farther west into Telemark Hollow.

5. Telemark Hollow

The Trans-Wasatch Company acquired Park City Consolidated's canyon mining property with plans to build residential units here, clustered in small villages, with ski lifts and resort buildings. Deer Valley residents on the other end of the hollow opposed the development. Deer Valley is a residential cul-de-sac with no present outlet

Jordanelle Reservoir (VI. 4)

besides Deer Valley Drive. Telemark Hollow developers originally intended to expand and pave Heber Avenue, but the Park City Council, in concert with Deer Valley residents, blocked this improvement. Trans-Wasatch subsequently sued for $12 million, alleging the city reneged on an old mining company agreement allowing improvements. The city argues that permission was given to grade, not to pave. After a series of legal negotiations, a compromise for development is being worked out.

If you are fatigued by this gradual but steady climb to McKinley Gap, there are pleasant areas along the way for breaks among the aspens and wild flowers. When you encounter a level area, a short dip, then another gradual climb next to a string of telephone poles, you are a little over halfway to the top.

After a McKinley Gap trail sign, you will be treated to a spectacular view of Deer Valley. The elevation here is 7,312 feet. You have climbed about 1,000 feet.

6. Deer Valley Resort

Descending from high mountain aspen groves, you will enter an upscale vacation-home mecca. During Park City's early years Deer Valley was an agricultural area that supported slaughter yards and fish ponds. The Daly-Judge Mine operated a zinc mill on the valley's south-eastern side. The ski area in the mountains now encompasses what once was the earliest Park City miners' camp at Lake Flat.

The Royal Street Company led by Edgar Stern bought the Park City Ski resort and Deer Valley real estate in the 1970s. Stern's grandfather was a co-founder of Sears & Roebuck, and Stern himself invested widely in communications and real estate including some in Aspen, Colorado. He lost the Park City Ski Resort in the mid-1970s economic recession but managed to hold on to Deer Valley. Opening for business in 1982, Stern's Deer Valley Resort soon became the area's most trendy playground. Dr. Art Ulene, of television's *Today Show,* was "resident physician" during the 1980s. In the hills above Deer Valley sits Stein Eriksen's more exclusive namesake lodge, including the Glittretind restaurant, and the neighboring Silver Lake Lodge Resort.

In 1994 Deer Valley Resort proposed doubling its skiing capacity with new lifts and slopes extending to Empire Ridge and bringing it close to Park City resort. Deer Valley hopes that more difficult ski runs will change its image as a beginner/intermediate resort. With the current rate of development, skiers may eventually be able to start their runs near Jordanelle and ski all the way to Wolf Mountain on the other side of Park City.

The resort development was hit by monkey-wrenchers in 1993. Environmentalists destroyed equipment employed in constructing new runs and lifts. These eco-warriors poured sugar into fuel lines, destroyed hydraulics and computer systems, smashed windshields, and graffitied "2 Much 2 Soon" and "Stop this Overdevelopment" on tractor

Deer Valley (VI. 6)

shovels. Similar vandalism occurs on occasion at the Winter Sports Olympic Park construction site.

Follow Heber Avenue as it descends the hill into Deer Valley to exit onto Queen Esther Drive, named for another of Park City's famous mining claims. Turn left onto Queen Esther, passing Amundsen Court, Gilt Edge Circle, and Good Trump Court, winding to the south and then west to Deer Valley Drive.

Turn left and follow Deer Valley Drive as it curves past the pond and gazebo to your right, followed by the lower resort parking lots. To your left are the Deer Valley Resort lodges.

Opposite the Comstock Lodge on your left, at the "Lot 5" sign on your right, is a paved one-way lane that runs between the lots. Pause briefly here to notice how Deer Valley Drive continues south and loops around at the end of the valley in front of Snow Park Lodge and the four principal ski lifts. When the Utah Symphony holds its summer concerts on the grassy expanse between the lifts, the sloping amphitheater becomes dotted with concert goers on blankets with picnic dinners.

Turn right onto the one-way lane that runs between the parking lots and ride the short distance to the intersection with a stop sign (there is a one-way sign and a "to Park City" arrow here as well). This is, of course, still Deer Valley Drive. Across the street to your left, below the retaining walls, is Royal Street which leads to Stein Eriksen and Silver Lake lodges and the exclusive American Flag and Bald Eagle residential developments, including the ski-vacation homes of many Hollywood celebrities.

Turn right and head north past the Lakeside development on your right and the Aspen Wood on your left. Immediately following the Deer Valley Plaza, where the popular Stew Pot Restaurant is located, the two forks of Deer Valley Drive converge again just after a short bridge with stone walls.

At this point carefully cross over to the paved bicycle path on the west side of the street where you will see a yellow "bikeway narrows" sign and two cast-iron vents. Follow the bicycle path north, veering gradually west, alongside Silver Creek to your left and Deer Valley Drive to your right. You will pass Stonebridge Lane, Rossie Hill Drive, and Deer Valley Loop on your way to the intersection with Marsac Avenue.

Between Deer Valley Loop and Marsac Avenue is a historic marker to your left next to a "bikeway narrows" sign. As the marker notes, this was once Park City's red light district.

7. The Row

Prostitutes held forth here on the outskirts of town from the earliest days. The block was euphemistically known as "The Row." In 1910 five bawdy houses were situated here, the establishments of Opal Crawford, Lydia de Garmo, Daisy Hubbard, Frankie Miller, and the infamous Rachel Urban. In 1908, when Rachel married George Urban, a carpenter, she already had six children. She later became wealthy and drove a hired limousine.

City police held regular raids on the Row, and its tenants were rounded up, brought into court, and charged the standard fine of $25, which the women counted as another business cost. "Bessie's," the last surviving Row house, closed in 1956 and burned down in 1970.

Prostitutes weren't allowed to visit town. Consequently, an understanding of the mysteries of the Row became part of a Park City upbringing. Park native Gay Kummer recalled delivering newspapers on the Row and her enchantment with the fashions, hairdos, and perfumes of its residents. Her mother slapped her when she asked about these women and forbade her to return with any more papers.

Continue to Marsac Avenue, another route to Stein Eriksen Lodge and Guardsman Pass, a road (closed in winter) for four-wheel-drive vehicles, leading to the Brighton and Solitude ski areas in Big Cottonwood Canyon in the Salt Lake Valley. Notice that Marsac Avenue makes a T-intersection of sorts with Deer Valley Drive which cuts a 45-degree corner and continues in a northwesterly direction. Carefully cross over Marsac Avenue to the continuation of the bike path and head north. Keep on the concrete, following the arrow to "City Park." The "Poison Creek Parkway" was planned originally in 1980 through the crusading work of Marianne Cone, Harry Reed, and Bill Coleman.

At Heber Avenue you will come to a stop sign. Cross Heber to the north, continuing on the path paralleling Deer Valley Drive and Silver Creek to your right. To your left you will see lower Main Street, the Park Station Condominium Hotel, and Miners Hospital and city park. You will then pass under Deer Valley Drive and ride past a cluster of small buildings, including a sports medicine clinic, to emerge at the intersection of Bonanza and Iron Horse drives.

As you exit the path, cross Iron Horse north to the sidewalk, proceed east a few yards to the corner, and turn left without crossing Bonanza. Ride north on Bonanza a short distance to the pedestrian crossing. Carefully cross Bonanza to the east and follow the dirt and gravel path alongside Silver Creek to the gazebo ahead to your left, just above the parking lot where you began. This ends the Telemark Hollow bicycle tour.

Bibliography

Biele, Katherine. "The Queen of Dough." *Salt Lake City Magazine*, May-June 1994, 60-65.

City Justice's Court Records, Park City, Summit County, Utah (microfilm). Utah State Historical Society, Salt Lake City.

Goddard, Stephen B. *Getting There: The Epic Struggle between Road and Rail in the American Century.* New York: Basic Books, 1994.

Gomes, Teri. "Park City's Tough Choices." *Utah Holiday*, Mar. 1985, 43-45.

Greever, William S. *Bonanza West: The Story of the Western Mining Rushes, 1848-1900.* Moscow: University of Idaho Press, 1993.

Historic Preservation Office. "Structure/Site Information Forms." Utah State Historical Society, Salt Lake City.

The Lodestar. Park City, UT: 1977- .

Leach, William. *Land of Desire: Merchants, Power and the Rise of a New American Culture.* New York: Random House, 1993.

Milner, Clyde, et. al., eds. *Oxford History of the American West.* New York: Oxford University Press, 1994.

Park City, Utah, 1902: The Past, Present and Future Souvenir Edition. Park City, UT: Park Record, 1902.

Park Record. Park City, UT: 1878- .

Pointer, Larry. *In Search of Butch Cassidy.* Norman: University of Oklahoma Press, 1977.

Randall, Deborah Lyn. "Park City, Utah: An Architectural History of Mining Town Housing, 1869-1907." M.A. thesis, University of Utah, 1985.

Ringholz, Raye Carlson. *Diggings and Doings in Park City.* N.p., 1983.

———. *Park City Trails.* Salt Lake City: Wasatch Publishers, Inc., 1984.

———, and Bea Kummer. *Walking through Historic Park City.* N.p., 1984.

Sanborn Insurance Maps, Park City, Utah. Special Collections, Marriott Library, University of Utah.

Smith, Duane A. *Mining America: The Industry and the Environment, 1800-1980.* Niwot: University of Colorado Press, 1993.

Spence, Clark C. *Mining Engineers and the American West: The Lace-Boot Brigade, 1849-1933.* Moscow: University of Idaho Press, 1993.

Thompson, George A., and Fraser Buck. *Treasure Mountain Home: Park City Revisited.* Salt Lake City: Dream Garden Press, 1993.

United States Census, Summit County, 1880, 1900, 1910, 1920. LDS Church Family History Library, Salt Lake City.

United States Department of the Interior, National Park Service. "National Register of Historic Places Inventory—Nomination Forms." Utah State Historical Society, Salt Lake City.

United States Geological Survey. "Topographical Maps." Utah State Historical Society, Salt Lake City.

West, Elliott. *The Saloon and the Rocky Mountain Frontier*. Lincoln: University of Nebraska Press, 1979.

Wright, Dean Franklin. "A History of Park City, 1869 to 1898." M.A. thesis, University of Utah, 1971.

Glossary

VERNACULAR STYLE

four-square, hipped-roof
("Pyramid House")

rectangular plan
("Hall & Parlor Cabin")

VERNACULAR STYLE

cross-wing plan
(" T- Cottage")

shotgun plan
("Vertical Cabin")

ROOFS

gable

salt box

pyramid

cupola

dormer

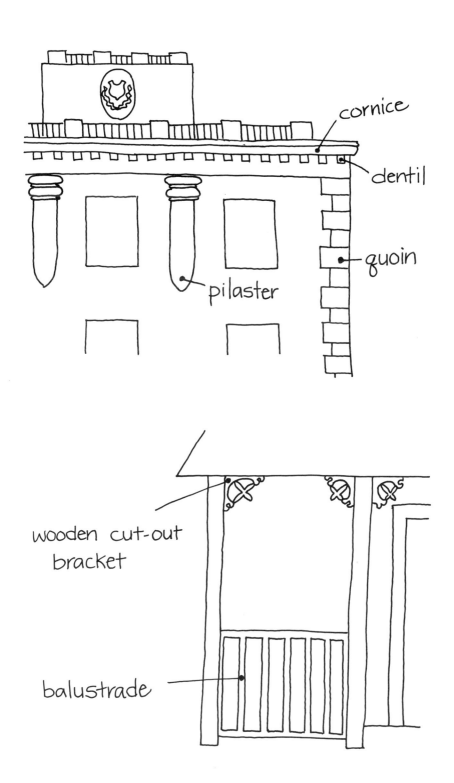

cornice

dentil

quoin

pilaster

wooden cut-out
bracket

balustrade

WALLS

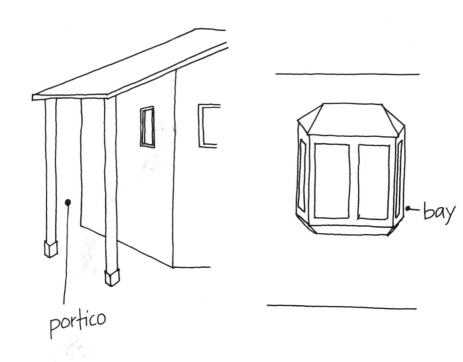

portico

bay

WINDOWS

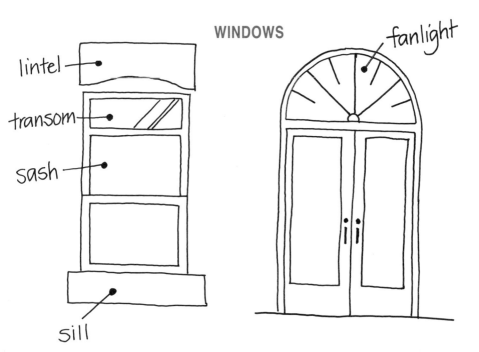

lintel

transom

sash

sill

fanlight